CLARENCE S. DARROW

RESIST NOT EVIL

Judge not, that ye be not judged.
Matthew 7:1.

Ye have heard that it hath been said: An eye for an eye, and a tooth for a tooth. But I say unto you, that ye resist not evil, but whosoever shall smite thee on thy right cheek, turn to him the other also.
Matthew 5:38, 39.

CONTENTS

THE TIMELESS WISDOM COLLECTION

Emerson once said: *"Consider what you have in the smallest chosen library. A company of the wisest and wittiest men that could be picked out of all civil countries in a thousand years, have set in best order the results of their learning and wisdom. The men themselves were hid and inaccessible, solitary, impatient of interruptions, fenced by etiquette; but the thought which they did not uncover to their bosom friend is here written out in transparent words to us, the strangers of another age."*

TWC is YOUR small library. Thousands of individual books and anthologies, the best of the best in fiction and non-fiction from the 19th and 20th Centuries, written by men and women whose lives were committed to enlighten the world with the wisdom of the ages.

Our fiction features names as Hemingway, Faulkner, Wells, Orwell, Huxley, Doyle, Twain, Burroughs, Chesterton, Alcott, C. S. Lewis, J. M. Barrie, Edgar Wallace, and hundreds more... Authors who have enriched our lives and forever enlarged our capacity to dream, to get enamoured by the characters, to suffer their pain, tragedies, and triumphs as if they were ours; as if they were true...

In self-development and positive-thinking, our authors include Napoleon Hill, Dale Carnegie, Charles Haanel, William Atkinson, Orison Swett Marden, Wallace Wattles, James Allen, Christian D. Larson, Florence Scovell-Shinn, Robert Collier and many more.

In Psychology, we have the works of Freud, Jung, Coué, Coriat, Adler and many others; and in philosophy, the works of Kant, Russell, Whitehead and Eucken, among others. In theosophy and mysticism, our authors include Blavatsky, Bulwer, Besant, Leadbeater, and Sinnet. We feature the works of scientists as Eddington, Darwin, and J.W.Dunne; successful industrialists as Henry Ford, Andrew Carnegie and Charles Schwab; and Economists as John Maynard Keynes...

Thousands of carefully selected masterpieces that have brilliantly captured the essence of life, are now being placed in your hands. *The results of the learning and wisdom of the greatest minds, set in best order,* as Emerson would say. Books for enlightenment, learning, illumination... that will provide the seeker –the one who is ready and is paying attention–, some of the deepest answers to life.

Mauricio Chaves-Mesén, Author of
12 Laws of Successful Entrepreneurs;
Think Success; and The Knights of Nostradamus

PREFACE

It is not claimed that the following pages contain any new ideas. They were inspired by the writings of Tolstoy, who was the first, and in fact the only, author of my acquaintance who ever seemed to me to place the doctrine of non-resistance upon a substantial basis. After reading Tolstoy I determined to make a careful study of the subject, but on a thorough search of book stores and libraries could find next to nothing dealing with the question, while the shelves were crowded with literature extolling the glories of war and the beneficence of patriotism.

The first part of this volume which deals with the state is very fragmentary, and in no wise so complete as can be found in many other volumes, but in the portion which deals with crime and punishment, I have found a much newer field, and one which has generally been discussed by those who have little practical knowledge of the machinery of courts of justice.

It has been my purpose to state the reasons which appeal to me in support of the doctrine of non-resistance, rather than to give authorities to sustain the theories advanced. Still, I believe that the student who is interested in the subject of criminology, and wishes to carefully investigate crime and punishment, will find that most of the great historians, philosophers, and thinkers will amply corroborate the views herein set forth, as to the cause of crime, and the evil and unsatisfactory results of punishment.

Clarence S. Darrow.

Chicago, November 1, 1902.

CHAPTER I.

THE NATURE OF THE STATE

In this heroic age, given to war and conquest and violence, the precepts of peace and good will seem to have been almost submerged. The pulpit, the press, and the school unite in teaching patriotism and in proclaiming the glory and beneficence of war; and one may search literature almost in vain for one note of that "Peace on earth, and good will toward men" in which the world still professes to believe; and yet these benign precepts are supposed to be the basis of all the civilization of the western world.

The doctrine of non-resistance, if ever referred to, is treated with derision and scorn. At its best the doctrine can only be held by dreamers and theorists, and can have no place in daily life. Every government on earth furnishes proof that there is nothing practical or vital in its teachings. Every government on earth is the personification of violence and force, and yet the doctrine of non-resistance is as old as human thought—even more than this, the instinct is as old as life upon the earth.

The doctrine of non-resistance to evil does not rest upon the words of Christ alone. Buddha, Confucius, Plato, Socrates, show the evil and destruction of war, of conquest, of violence, and of hatred, and have taught the beneficence of peace, of forgiveness, of non-resistance to evil. But modern thought is not content to rest the conduct of life upon the theories of moralists. The rules of life that govern men and states must today be in keeping with science and conform to the highest reason and judgment of man. It is here that non-resistance seems to have failed to make any practical progress in the world. That men should "turn the other cheek," should "love their enemies," should "resist not evil," has ever seemed fine to teach to children, to preach on Sundays, to round a period in a senseless oratorical flight; but it has been taken for granted that these sentiments cannot furnish the real foundation for strong characters or great states.

It is idle to discuss "non-resistance" in its effect upon life and the world without adopting some standard of excellence by which to judge results. Here, as elsewhere in human conduct, after all is said and done, men must come back to the fundamental principle that the conduct which makes for life is wise and right. Nature in her tireless labor has ever been developing a higher order and a completer life. Sometimes for long periods it seems as if the world were on the backward course, but even this would prove that life really is the highest end to be attained. Whatever tends to happiness tends to life,—joy is life and misery is death.

In his long and toilsome pilgrimage, man has come to his present estate through endless struggle, through brutal violence administered and received. And the question of the correctness of non-resistance as a theory, like any other theory, does not depend upon whether it can be enforced and lived now or tomorrow, but whether it is the highest ideal of life that is given us to conceive. In one sense nothing is practical excepting what is; everything must have been developed out of all the conditions of life that now exist or have existed on the earth. But to state this means little in the settlement of ethical questions, for man's future condition depends quite as much upon his mental attitude as upon any other fact that shapes his course.

Everywhere it seems to have been taken for granted that force and violence are necessary to man's welfare upon the earth. Endless volumes have been written, and countless lives been sacrificed in an effort to prove that one form of government is better than another; but few seem seriously to have considered the proposition that all government rests on violence and force, is sustained by soldiers, policemen and courts, and is contrary to the ideal peace and order which make for the happiness and progress of the human race. Now and then it is even admitted that in the far distant ages yet to come men may so far develop toward the angelic that political governments will have no need to be. This admission, like the common concept, presumes that governments are good; that their duties undertaken and performed consist in repressing the evil and the lawless, and protecting and caring for the helpless and the weak.

If the history of the state proved that governing bodies were ever formed for this purpose or filled this function, there might be some basis for the assumption that government is necessary to preserve order and to defend the weak. But the origin and evolution of the political state show quite another thing—it shows that the state was born in aggression, and that in all the various stages through which it has passed its essential characteristics have been preserved.

The beginnings of the state can be traced back to the early history of the human race when the strongest savage seized the largest club and with this weapon enforced his rule upon the other members of the tribe. By means of strength and cunning he became the chief and exercised this power, not to protect the weak but to take the good things of the earth for himself and his. One man by his unaided strength could not long keep the tribe in subjection to his will, so he chose lieutenants and aides, and these too were taken for their strength and prowess, and were given a goodly portion of the fruits of power for the loyalty and help they lent their chief. No plans for the general good ever formed a portion of the scheme of government evolved by these barbarous chiefs. The great mass were slaves, and their lives and liberty held at the absolute disposal of the strong.

Ages of evolution have only modified the rigors of the first rude states. The divine right to rule, the absolute character of official power, is practically the same today in most of the nations of the world as with the early chiefs who executed their mandates with a club. The ancient knight who, with battle-axe and coat of mail, enforced his rule upon the weak, was only the forerunner of the tax-gatherer and tax-devourer of today. Even in democratic countries, where the people are supposed to choose their rulers, the nature of government is the same. Growing from the old ideas of absolute power, these democracies have assumed that some sort of government was indispensable to the mass, and no sooner had they thrown off one form of bondage than another yoke was placed upon their necks, only to prove in time that this new burden was no less galling than the old. Neither do the people govern in democracies more than in any other lands. They do not even choose their rulers. These rulers choose themselves and by force and cunning and intrigue arrive at the same results that their primitive ancestor reached with the aid of a club.

And who are these rulers without whose aid the evil and corrupt would destroy and subvert the defenceless and the weak? From the earliest time these self-appointed rulers have been conspicuous for all those vices that they so persistently charge to the common people whose rapacity, cruelty and lawlessness they so bravely curb. The history of the past and the present alike proves beyond a doubt that if there is, or ever was any large class, from whom society needed to be saved, it is those same rulers who have been placed in absolute charge of the lives and destinies of their fellow men. From the early kings who, with blood-red hands, forbade their subjects to kill their fellow men, to the modern legislator, who, with the bribe money in his pocket, still makes bribery a crime, these rulers have ever made laws not to govern themselves but to enforce obedience on their serfs.

The purpose of this autocratic power has ever been the same. In the early tribe the chief took the land and the fruits of the earth, and parceled them amongst his retainers who helped preserve his strength. Every government since then has used its power to divide the earth amongst the favored few and by force and violence to keep the toiling, patient, suffering millions from any portion of the common bounties of the world.

In many of the nations of the earth the real governing power has stood behind the throne, has suffered their creatures and their puppets to be the nominal rulers of nations and states, but in every case the real rulers are the strong, and the state is used by them to perpetuate their power and serve their avarice and greed.

CHAPTER II

ARMIES AND NAVIES

How is the authority of the state maintained? In whatever guise, or however far removed from the rudest savage tribe to the most modern democratic state, this autocratic power rests on violence and force alone. The first great instrument which supports every government on earth is the soldier with his gun and sword. True, the army may be but rarely used. The civil power, the courts of justice, the policemen and jails generally suffice in civilized lands to maintain existing things; but back of these, to enforce each decree, is the power of armed men with all the modern implements of death.

Thousands of church organizations throughout the Christian world profess the doctrine of non-resistance to evil, of peace on earth and good will to men, and yet each of these Christian lands trains great bodies of armed men to kill their fellows for the preservation of existing things. Europe is made up of great military camps where millions of men are kept apart from their fellows and taught the trade of war alone. And democratic America, feeling the flush of victory and the glow of conquest, is turning her energies and strength to gathering armies and navies that shall equal those across the sea. Not only are these trained soldiers a living denial of the doctrines that are professed, but in obedience to an eternal law, deeper and more beneficent than any ever made by man, these mighty forces are working their own ruin and death. These great armies and navies which give the lie to our professions of faith exist for two purposes: first, to keep in subjection the people of their own land; second, to make war upon and defend against the other nations of the earth. The history of the world is little else than the story of the carnage and destruction wrought on battlefields; carnage and destruction springing not from any difference between the common people of the earth, but due alone to the desires and passions of the rulers of the earth. This ruling class, ever eager to extend its power and strength, ever looking for new people to govern and new lands to tax, has always been ready to turn its face against other powers to satisfy the ruler's will, and without pity or regret, these rulers have depopulated their kingdoms, and carried ruin and destruction to every portion of the earth for gold and power.

Not only do these European rulers keep many millions of men whose only trade is war, but these must be supported in worse than useless idleness by the labor of the poor. Still other millions are trained to war and are ever ready to answer to their master's call, to desert their homes and trades and offer up their lives to satisfy the vain ambitions of the ruler of the state. Millions more must give their strength and lives to build forts and ships, make guns and cannon and all the modern implements of war. Apart from any moral question of the right of man to slay his fellow man, all this great burden rests upon the poor. The vast expense of war comes from the production of the land and must serve to weaken and impair its industrial strength. This very force must destroy itself. The best talent of every nation is called upon to invent new implements of destruction—faster sailing boats, stronger forts, more powerful explosives and more deadly guns. As one nation adds to its military stores, so every other nation is also bound to increase its army and navy too. Thus the added force does not augment the military power, but only makes larger the burden of the state; until, today, these great armies, aside from producing the moral degradation of the world, are sapping and undermining and consuming the vitality and strength of all the nations of the earth. Cost of labor and strength means cost of life. Thus in their practical results these armies are destroying millions of lives that a policy of peace and non-resistance would conserve and save.

But when these armies are in action how stands the case? Over and over again the world has been submerged by war. The strongest nations of the earth have been almost destroyed. Devastating wars have left consequences that centuries could not repair. Countless millions of men have been used as food for guns. The miseries and sufferings and brutality following in the wake of war have never been described or imagined, and yet the world persists in teaching the glory and honor and greatness of war. To excuse the wholesale butcheries of men by the governing powers, learned apologists have taught that without the havoc and cruel devastation of war the human race would overrun the earth; and yet every government in the world has used its power and influence to promote and encourage marriage and the rearing of children, to punish infanticide and abortion, and make criminal every device to prevent population; have used their power to heal the sick, to alleviate misery and to prolong life. Every movement to overcome disease, to make cities sanitary, to produce and maintain men and women and children has received the sanction and encouragement of all governments; and still these glorious rulers have ruthlessly slaughtered in the most barbarous and cruel way tens of millions of their fellow men, to add to their glory and perpetuate their names. And philosophers have told us that this was necessary to prevent the over-population of the earth!

No single ruler, however cruel or ambitious, has ever yet been able to bring the whole world beneath his sway, and the ambitions and lusts of these separate chiefs have divided the world into hostile camps and hostile states. Endless wars have been waged to increase or protect the territory governed by these various rulers. In these bloody conflicts the poor serfs have dumbly and patiently met death in a thousand sickening ways to uphold the authority and prowess of the ruler whose sole function has ever been to pillage and rob the poor victims that fate has placed within his power. To these brutal, senseless, fighting millions the boundaries of the state or the color of the flag that they were taught to love could not in the least affect their lives. Whoever their rulers, their mission has ever been to toil and fight and die for the honor of the state and the glory of the chief.

But, today, even national preservation demands that the rule of peace shall give place to the rule of war. In the older countries of the earth the great drains made upon industry and life to support vast armies and equip them for slaughter is depopulating states and impoverishing the lands. And besides all this, so far as external power is concerned, no nation adds to its effectiveness to battle with the others by increasing its army and navy. This simply serves to increase the strength of the enemy's guns and to make new combinations between hostile lands, until the very strength of a nation becomes its weakness and must in turn lead to its decay and overthrow. The nation that would today disarm its soldiers and turn its people to the paths of peace would accomplish more to its building up than by all the war taxes wrung from its hostile and unwilling serfs. A nation like this would exhibit to the world such an example of moral grandeur and true vitality and worth that no nation, however powerful, would dare to invite the odium and hostility of the world by sending arms and men to conquer a peaceful, productive, non-resistant land. If the integrity and independence of a nation depended upon its forts and guns the smaller countries of Europe would at once be wiped from the map of the world. Switzerland, Holland, Greece, Italy, and Spain are absolutely powerless to defend themselves by force. If these nations should at once disarm every soldier and melt every gun and turn the worse than wasted labor into productive, life-saving work, they could but greatly strengthen themselves amongst the other nations of the earth. Not only this, their example would serve to help turn the tide of the world from the barbarous and soul-destroying path of war toward the higher, nobler life of peace and good will toward men.

But not alone are these small nations made still weaker by war, but every battleship that is built by England, Russia, France, Germany, or the United States really weakens those nations too. It weakens them not alone by the loss of productive power but by the worse than wasted energy which is required to support these implements of death, from the time their first beam is mined in the original ore, until scarred and worthless and racked by scenes of blood and violence and shame, they are thrown out upon the sands to rot. But every battleship weakens a nation by inviting the hostility of the other peoples of the earth, by compelling other rulers to weaken their kingdoms, to build mighty ships and powerful guns. Every preparation for war and violence is really a violation of the neutrality under which great nations profess to live. They are a reflection upon the integrity and humanity of their own people and an insult to every other land on earth. The building of a man of war, the rearing of a fort, or the planting of a gun can be likened only to a man who professes to live in peace and quiet with his neighbors and his friends and who goes about armed with pistol and with dirk.

But these patent evils and outrages are after all the smallest that flow from violence and strife. The whole pursuit of war weakens the aspirations and ideals of the race. Rulers have ever taught and encouraged the spirit of patriotism, that they might call upon their slaves to give their labor to the privileged class and to freely offer up their lives when the king commands. Every people in the world is taught that their country and their government is the best on earth, and that they should be ever ready to desert their homes, abandon their hopes, aspirations, and ambitions when their ruler calls, and this regardless of the right or wrong for which they fight. The teaching of patriotism and war permeates all society, it reaches to the youngest child and even shapes the character of the unborn babe. It fills the soul with false ambitions, with ignoble desires, and with sordid hopes.

Every sentiment for the improvement of men, for human justice, for the uplifting of the poor, is at once stifled by the wild, hoarse shout for blood. The lowest standard of ethics of which a right-thinking man can possibly conceive is taught to the common soldier whose trade is to shoot his fellow man. In youth he may have learned the command, "Thou shalt not kill," but the ruler takes the boy just as he enters manhood and teaches him that his highest duty is to shoot a bullet through his neighbor's heart,—and this unmoved by passion or feeling or hatred, and without the least regard to right or wrong, but simply because his ruler gives the word. It is not the privilege of the common soldier to ask questions, to consider right and wrong, to think of the misery and suffering his act entails upon others innocent of crime. He may be told to point his gun at his neighbor and his friend, even at his brother or father; if so he must obey commands.

Theirs not to reason why,

Theirs but to do and die,

represents the code of ethics that governs a soldier's life.

And yet from men who believe in these ideals, men who sacrifice their right of private judgment in the holiest matter that can weigh upon the conscience and the intellect, the taking of human life,—men who place their lives, their consciences, their destinies, without question or hesitation, into another's keeping, men whose trade is slaughter and whose cunning consists in their ability to kill their fellows,—from such men it is expected to build great states and rear a noble humanity!

These teachings lead to destruction and death; the destruction of the body and the destruction of the soul. Even on the plea of physical evolution in the long sweep of time, these men must give way to the patient, peaceful, non-resistants, who love their brothers and believe in the sacredness of life. Long ago it was written down that "He who takes the sword shall perish by the sword."

CHAPTER III

THE PURPOSE OF ARMIES

But the great armies and navies are not really kept today for foreign conquest. Now and then, in obedience to the commercial spirit that rules the world, these vessels of destruction are sent to foreign seas. But the rulers of the earth live on fairly friendly terms. Long since, the most ambitious have abandoned their dreams of world power and are content to exploit a portion of the earth. When warships are sent to foreign seas they usually fire a salute rather than train their guns for death. Monarchs the world over respect each other. They are bound together by ties of common interest, if not of common love. When a ruler dies, even though the most tyrannical and despotic, every other ruler promptly sends condolences to the sorrowing court; their own subjects may die unwept, but a touch of common feeling moves them to mourn a ruler's death. Nations are bound by many ties to preserve peace among each other. Scions of royal families are handed round in marriage from court to court, treaties of all sorts are made and ratified in most solemn form; and even more than this, the real owners of the world, those who possess the stocks and bonds which rest upon the wealth that the poor have labored to create, these real rulers who make war or peace by giving or withholding funds, these own the great bulk of the property of the various nations of the world, and will not lightly suffer their possessions to be destroyed. And yet these same real rulers, who stand behind the thrones of all the world, approve of this preparation for war, approve of taking millions of men from their homes and training them to kill, approve of every fort and gun and battleship. More than this, they contribute largely of their private funds to build batteries and equip militia, especially in the great cities of the earth. Through the speeches of their agents and the voice of their press, all this grim visage of war is for the stranger without their gates. But in reality the prime reason for all the armies of the world is that soldiers and militia may turn their guns upon their unfortunate countrymen when the owners of the earth shall speak the word. And these unfortunate countrymen are the outcast and despised, the meek and lowly ones of the world, the men whose ceaseless toil and unpaid efforts have built the forts and molded the cannon and sustained the soldiers that are used to shoot them down.

To say that these armies and frowning forts and Gatling guns are needed to maintain peace and order at home is to admit at once that the great mass of men are held captive by the more powerful few. Organized soldiers and policemen, courts and sheriffs, with guns and forts and jails, have the greatest advantage over the disorganized mass who cannot act together, and who know not which way to turn to keep outside the meshes of the law. Not one in a thousand need be trained to arms and authority to keep the unorganized mass in the place reserved for it to live. The purpose of guns and armies is to furnish the few an easy and sure way to control the mass. Neither are these armies made of the ruling class. The officers, it is true, are generally taken from the favored ones, but the regular soldier is the man too poor and abandoned to find his place in any other of the walks of life. He is only fit to be an executioner of his fellow man. No ruler can love his subjects when he takes their money and their labor to buy cannon and train men to shoot them down. That this is the real purpose of standing armies and warlike equipments is plain to all who have eyes to see. More and more the rulers have learned to build their barracks and mass their troops not on the borders of their land but convenient to great cities, in the midst of districts thickly populated by working men. As nations grow older the opportunities of the masses grow less. More men are called to serve the state, and greater preparations are made to preserve the possessions of the rich. These soldiers are moved from place to place, are massed at time of need, not in accordance with the petition of the citizens from whose ranks the soldiers come, but in response to the request of the ruling class.

Quite apart from the question of the rights of capital on one hand and labor on the other, what must be the effect of this policy of force and violence when reaching over long periods of time? A nation is really great and possessed of the lasting elements of strength in proportion as her people are strong, intelligent, and free. The rulers of a nation should owe their subjects some duty in return for the homage and taxes they receive. The ruler who deliberately governs his subjects by violence and force, and through tyranny and fear, must find in time that this policy of hatred and outrage is destroying and sapping the foundations of the state; the more strength and vitality that he draws from the poor and the more soldiers required to support arbitrary power, the greater the chasm that yawns beneath his feet. The loyalty that is kept through fear is lost with opportunity. The rulers of Rome before her destruction, and of France before the Revolution, had drawn all the soldiers from the people that the fields and shops could spare, and used these to support their tottering power. Kings can gain nothing by governing soldiers alone. They must have farmers, artisans, all sorts of producers, or their conquest is not worth the price. The policy of hatred and violence must in the end destroy the state. It can breed only hatred in the hearts of the outcast and the poor. If their subjection is incomplete, the throne is resting upon the shifting sands. If perfect and complete, their subjects are lifeless machines and their empires crumbling to decay. It is really idle to speculate as to whether love and brotherhood could accomplish more; it is certain they could not do less. To disband the armies and destroy the forts, to diffuse love and brotherhood, and peace and justice in the place of war and strife, could tend only to the building up of character, the elevation of the soul, and the strength and well-being of the state. True, the class lines would disappear. Brotherhood would have neither ruler nor ruled, would have no authority of man over man, would treat all as brothers and co-equals, and from it would grow a stronger state and a higher manhood than the world has known. Peaceful industry relieved from the burdens of soldiers and arms would inevitably increase, and life, rendered less burdensome by the exactions of authority, would lengthen and sweeten through the beneficent influence of love. No nation can be really great that is held together by Gatling guns, and no true loyalty can be induced and kept through fear.

CHAPTER IV

CIVIL GOVERNMENT

After the evolution of society through brute force and the first stages of militarism, comes civil government. In its forms and methods civil government differs from military government, but in its essence, its real purpose and effect, it is the same. Civil government, like military government, rests on violence and force. As society reaches the industrial stage, it is easier and costs less waste of energy for the ruling class to maintain its supremacy through the intricate forms and mazes of civil government, than through the direct means of soldiers and guns.

Civil governments, like military governments, are instituted and controlled by the ruling class. Their purpose is to keep the earth and its resources in the hands of those who directly and indirectly have taken it for themselves. This can only be done by the establishment and maintenance of certain rules and regulations concerning the disposition of property and the fate of men. A vast army of officials, governors, legislators, tax-gatherers, judges, sheriffs, policemen, and the like are maintained by the governing class to enforce these rules and regulations and keep the exploited in their place. The decrees of courts and the various orders of civil government are enforced by violence, differing only in kind from the general's commands. The decrees of courts, whether rightful or wrongful, must be obeyed, and the penalty of disobedience is the forcible taking of property, the kidnapping and imprisoning of men, and if need be, the taking of human life. If it shall ever occur that the civil authorities have not sufficient force to compel obedience, the whole power of the army and navy may at once be made subservient to the civil power.

The vast army which is charged with enforcing and maintaining civil law is drawn largely from the ruling class and those who contribute as their willing tools. This class must be supported and maintained in greater luxury than that enjoyed by the ordinary man, and the support entails ceaseless and burdensome exactions from the producing class. These exactions are a portion of the price that the worker pays for the privilege of being ruled. It is true that a portion of the money forcibly taken through the machinery of government is used for those cooperative commercial purposes that are incident to a complex social life, but it has never yet been shown that an autocratic power like a political state is needed to provide the common resources incident to social life.

Practically the whole army of officials, with its wastefulness, its extravagance and its endless peculation, is supported and kept in worse than idleness for the purpose of ruling men through violence and force. Even in so-called democracies the civil law, with its ponderous and costly machinery, serves the same purpose as in monarchical states. It is easy to understand that when the decrees of a ruler are absolute it can matter little whether these decrees are issued to an army and carried out by force of the bayonet and gun, or whether they are crystallized into law and carried out by the orders of courts to be enforced by consigning troublesome and rebellious subjects to the prison or the block. In either event the will of the sovereign is law, and the law is made for the benefit of the ruler, not the ruled.

In democracies, the form is somewhat changed, but the results are not unlike. Every democracy begins with a great mass of regulations inherited from the autocratic powers that have gone before. These laws and customs are originally the same decrees that have gone forth from the absolute rulers of the earth, and every change in forms and institutions is based upon the old notions of property and rights that were made to serve the ruler and enslave the world.

Then, too, authority has the same effect on human nature whether in an absolute monarchy or a democracy, and the tendency of authority is ever to enlarge its bounds and to encroach upon the natural rights of those who have no power to protect themselves. The possession of authority and arbitrary power ever tends to tyranny, and when autocratic orders may be enforced by violence, liberty and life depend upon sufferance alone. A close community of interest naturally springs up between those circumstanced alike. The man who possesses one sort of power, as, for instance, political privilege, is very friendly to the class who possess another sort, as, for instance, wealth, and this community of interest naturally and invariably arrays all the privileged classes against the weak. The laws and regulations of a democracy tend no more to equality than those of a monarchy. Under a democratic government inequality of possession, of opportunity, of power, is quite as great as under absolute monarchies. Given the right to use force of man over man and the strongest force will succeed. You may forbid it in one direction, it will but find a new method to accomplish the same result, like the pent-up torrent that will find its outlet, in however circuitous a route it is obliged to move. The legislators who make laws come either from the ruling class or draw their honors, rewards, and emoluments from this class; and the statutes of the most democratic state are not unlike the dictates of the absolute monarch, and the decrees of both alike may be enforced by all the power and violence of the state. But laws do not execute themselves, and every official appointed or self-chosen to enforce the law either comes from or naturally gravitates toward the ruling class. Here again power grows by what it feeds on. Order is more important than liberty, and at all costs order must be enforced upon the many. The few have little need for law. Whatever is, is theirs, and may they not use their own to suit themselves? The business of the courts and officials is to enforce order upon the great mass who must depend upon the few for the means of life. To enforce order upon them means that they may only live in certain ways.

But admitting the orthodox view of government to be correct, then how stands the case? The great majority of mankind still believe in the utility of the state. They not only believe that society could not exist without the state, but likewise that this political institution exists and is maintained for the public good; that all its functions and activities in some mysterious way have been conferred upon it by the weaker class of society, and that it is administered to save this class from the ravages of the vicious and the strong. Of course, there are many humane officials, men who use their power to promote the public good, as they see and understand the public good. These, in common with the community, look upon the endless provisions of our penal code as being the magical power that keeps the state from dissolution and preserves the lives and property of men from the vicious and the bad. The idea of punishment, of violence, of force, is so interwoven with all our concepts of justice and social life that but few can conceive a society without force, without jails, without scaffolds, without the penal judgments of men. The thought never suggests itself to the common mind that nature, unaided by man's laws, can evolve social order, or that a community might live in measurable peace and security moved only by those natural instincts which form the basis and render possible communal life. To be sure, the world is full of evidence that order and security do not depend on legal inventions. From the wild horses on the plains, the flocks of birds, the swarming bees, the human society and association in new countries amongst unexploited people, suggestions of order and symmetry regulated by natural instincts and common social needs are ample to show the possibility at least of order or a considerable measure of justice without penal law. It is only when the arrogance and the avarice of rulers and chiefs make it necessary to exploit men that these rulers must lay down laws and regulations to control the actions of their fellows. And the more fixed the caste, the better settled the community; the more complete the private appropriation of land, and the longer the penal code, the greater the number of victims that are caught within its snares.

Turning from the examples everywhere present of the naturalness of order and system to what we observe of the daily acts of men, the thought that right conduct has little relation to penal laws is still further confirmed. In the myriad acts of men it is only rarely that one is done directly because of law. To turn to the right when you meet your neighbor on the street; to imperil your happiness and even your life to help in dire need; to protect the helpless; to defend the weak; to tell the truth; in fact, to obey all that natural morality or right conduct requires, is the first instinct of man, and ever prevails, not only regardless of human law but in spite of human law, and this, too, for the best and most abiding reason that can influence the life of man. Nature provides that certain conduct makes for life, and in the sweep of time, those who conform to this conduct live and their offspring populate the earth when they are gone; those who violate the laws of communal life will die or leave no descendants or weak offspring to be the last survivors of their line. The unschooled child and the uncivilized race alike tell the truth; they obey the laws of nature and the laws of life. It is only after the exploiter appears with his rules for enslaving man that he must needs build jails in which to pen those who defy or ignore their power.

CHAPTER V

THEORY OF CRIME AND PUNISHMENT

Those who believe in the beneficence of force have never yet agreed upon the crimes that should be forbidden, the method and extent of punishment, the purpose of punishment, nor even its result. They simply agree that without force and violence social life cannot be maintained. All conceivable human actions have fallen under the disfavor of the law and found their place in penal codes: blasphemy, witchcraft, heresy, insanity, idiocy, methods of eating and drinking, the manner of worshiping the Supreme Being, the observance of fast days and holy days, the giving of medicine and the withholding of medicine, the relation of the sexes, the right to labor and not to labor, the method of acquiring and dispensing property, its purchase and sale, the forms of dress and manner of deportment, in fact almost every conceivable act of man. On the other hand, murder, robbery, pillage, rapine, have often been commended by the ruling powers, not only permitted, but under certain conditions that seemed to work to the advantage of the ruler, this conduct has been deemed worthy of the greatest praise.

The punishment for illegal acts have been as various as the crimes. Death has always been a favorite visitation for the criminal, but the means of death have varied with time and place: boiling in oil, boiling in water, burning at the stake, breaking on the wheel, strangulation, poison, feeding to wild beasts, beheading, and in fact every conceivable way down to the humane method of electrocution and hanging by the neck until dead. Death, too, has been made the punishment for all sorts of crimes, always for the crimes of denying your Maker, or killing your ruler. After death, has come public flogging, standing in the stocks, ducking, maiming, down to the humane method of penning in a cage.

No two sets of rulers have ever agreed upon the relative enormity of the various crimes, the sort of punishment they merited, the extent and duration of punishment, or the purpose to be accomplished by the punishment. One age has pronounced martyrs and worshiped as saints the criminals that another age has put to death. One law-making body repeals the crimes that another creates. Some judges with venerable wigs have pronounced solemn sentence of death upon helpless, defenceless old women for bewitching a cat. Grave judges have even sentenced animals to death after due and impartial trial for crime. The judges who pronounced sentence of death on women for witchcraft were as learned and good as those who today pronounce sentence for conspiracy and other crimes. It is quite as possible that another generation will look with the same horror on the subjects of our laws as we look upon those of the years that are gone. It is but a few years since a hundred different crimes were punishable with death in England, and the wise men of that day would not have believed that the empire could hold together had these extreme statutes been limited to one or two.

But however drastic the laws at different periods of civilization, they have never been so broad but what a much larger number of blameworthy acts were outside than inside the code. Neither have they ever been enforced alike on all. The powerful could generally violate them with impunity, but the net was there to ensnare the victim whom they wished to catch.

Neither has the method of determining the victim for these various laws been as accurate and scientific as is generally presumed. Sometimes it has been by torturing until the victim is made to confess; sometimes by wager of battle; sometimes by tying the feet and hands and throwing them into a pond, when if they sank they were innocent, if they swam they were guilty and promptly put to death. The modern method of arraying a defendant in court, prosecuted by able lawyers with ample resources, tried by judges who almost invariably believe in the prisoner's guilt, defended as is usually the case by incompetent lawyers, and without means, is scarcely more liable to lead to correct results than the ancient forms. From the nature of things it is seldom possible to be sure about the commission of the act, and never possible to fix the moral responsibility of the person charged with crime. For ages men have erected scaffolds, instruments of torture, built jails, prisons and penal institutions without end, and through all the ages a long line of suffering humanity, bound and fettered, has been marching to slaughter and condemned to living tombs; and yet human governments charged with the responsibility of the condition and lives of these weak brothers, have never yet been able to agree even upon the purpose for which these pens are built. All punishment and violence is largely mixed with the feeling of revenge,—from the brutal father who strikes his helpless child, to the hangman who obeys the orders of the judge; with every man who lays violent unkind hands upon his fellow the prime feeling is that of hatred and revenge. Some human being has shed his neighbors blood; the state must take his life. In no other way can the crime be wiped away. In some inconceivable manner it is believed that when this punishment follows, justice has been done. But by no method of reasoning can it be shown that the injustice of killing one man is retrieved by the execution of another, or that the forcible taking of property is made right by confining some human being in a pen. If the law knew some method to restore a life or make good a loss to the real victim, it might be urged that justice had been done. But if taking life, or blaspheming, or destroying the property of another be an injustice, as in our short vision it seems to be, then punishing him who is supposed to be guilty of the act, in no way makes just the act already done.

To punish a human being simply because he has committed a wrongful act, without any thought of good to follow, is vengeance pure and simple, and more detestable and harmful than any casual isolated crime. Apologists who have seen the horror in the thought of vengeance and still believe in violence and force when exercised by the state, contend that punishment is largely for the purpose of reforming the victim. This, of course, cannot be held in those instances where death is the punishment inflicted. These victims at least have no chance to be reformed. Neither can it be seriously contended that a penal institution is a reformatory, whatever its name. A prisoner is an outlaw, an outcast man, placed beyond the pale of society and branded as unfit for the association of his fellow man; his sentence is to live in silence, to toil without recompense, to wear the badge of infamy, and if ever permitted to see the light to be pointed at and shunned by all who know his life.

CHAPTER VI

REMEDIAL EFFECTS OF PUNISHMENT

The last refuge of the apologist is that punishment is inflicted to prevent crime. No one can speak from experience as to whether punishment prevents what is called crime or not, for the experiment of non-resistance has never yet been fairly or fully tried. To justify killing or penning a human being upon the theory that this prevents crime should call for the strictest proof on the part of those who advocate this course. To take the life or liberty of a fellow man is the most serious responsibility that can devolve upon an individual or community. The theory that punishment is a preventive to unlawful acts does not seriously mean that it is administered to prevent the individual from committing a second or a third unlawful act. If this were the case the death penalty should never be inflicted, as life imprisonment accomplishes the same results. Neither would it be necessary to restrain men in the way that is done in our penal institutions, to deprive them of all pleasure and the income of their labor. All that would then be needed would be to keep men safely locked from the world. But most unlawful acts are committed hastily in the heat of passion or upon what seems adequate provocation, or through sore need. Such acts as these would almost never be repeated. Genuine repentance follows most really vicious acts, but repentance, however genuine, gives no waiver of punishment.

Then, too, many men who commit no act in violation of the law are known to be more likely to commit such acts than others who through some circumstances may have violated a criminal statute. Men of hasty temper, of strong will, of intemperate habits, often with no means of support, all of these are more liable to crime than one who has once overstepped the bounds. But it is obvious that this is not the real reason for punishment; if it were it would be the duty of judge and jury to determine, not whether a man had committed a crime, but whether he was liable to commit one at some future time, an inquiry which is never made and which it is obvious could not be made.

The safety aimed at through punishment is not meant the safety for the individual, but it is contended that the fact that one person is punished for an act deters others from the commission of similar unlawful acts; it is obvious that there is a large class who are not deterred by these examples, for the inmates of prisons never grow less, in fact prisons grow and increase in the same proportion as other institutions grow. But here, too, the theories and acts of rulers have been as various and contradictory as in relation to other matters concerning crime and its punishment. If the purpose of punishment is to terrorize the community so that none will dare again to commit these acts, then the more terrible the punishment the surer the result. This was generally admitted not many years ago, but in its treatment of crime the world ever prefers to be illogical and ineffectual rather than too brutal.

If terrorism is the object aimed at, death should again be substituted for the various crimes, great and small, which ever justified taking human life. Death, too, should be administered in the most cruel way. Boiling, the rack, wild beasts, and slow fires should be the methods sought. It should be steadfastly remembered by all squeamish judges and executioners that one vigorous punishment would prevent a thousand crimes. But more than all this, death should be in the most public way. The kettle of boiling oil should be heated with its victim inside, out upon the commons, where all eyes could see and all ears could hear. The scaffold should be erected high on a hill, and the occasion be made a public holiday for miles around. This was once the case even within the last half century. These public hangings in Europe and America have drawn great crowds of spectators, sometimes reaching into the tens of thousands, to witness the value that the state places on human life. But finally, even stupid legislators began to realize that these scenes of violence, brutality and crime bred their like upon those who came to see. Even governments discovered that many acts of violence followed a public hanging. The hatred of the state which calmly took a human life engendered endless hatred as its fruit. And in all countries that claim a semblance of civilization, public hangings are now looked back upon with horror and amazement. Hangings today take place inside the jail in the presence of a few invited guests, a state doctor who watches carefully to see that the victim is not cut down before his heart has ceased to beat, a chaplain who calls on the Creator of life to take back to his bosom the divine spark which man in his cruelty and wrath is seeking to snuff out. Even the state is not so cruel but that it will officially ask the Almighty to look after the soul that it blackens and defiles and does its best to everlastingly destroy. A few friends of the jailer are present to witness the rare performance, and the newspapers too are represented, so that the last detail, including the breakfast bill of fare, may be graphically set before the hungry mob to take the place of the real tragedy that they had the right to witness in the good old days. Many states today have provided that executions shall be inside the penitentiary walls, that the victim shall be wakened, if perchance he is asleep, in the darkness and dead of night; that he shall be hurried off alone and unobserved and hastily put to death outside the gaze of any curious eye; that this barbarism shall be done, this unholy, brutal deed committed in silence, in darkness, that the heavens and earth alike may cover up the shocking crime, from which a sensitive public conscience stands aghast. The ever-present public press in many cases is allowed to print only the barest details of the bloody scene, so that oblivion may the more quickly and deeply cover this crowning infamy of the state.

The abolition of public hangings may speak something for the sensitiveness, or at least, the squeamishness of the state. But it is evident that all of this is a terrible admission of guilt upon the part of those who uphold this crime. It is possible that one might believe at least in the sincerity of those who argue that punishment prevents crime, if these terrible scenes of violence were carried out in open day before the multitude, and fully understood and discussed in all their harrowing, shocking details of cruelty and blood. If the sight of punishment terrorizes men from the commission of crime then, of course, punishment should be as open as the day. In so far as the state is successful in keeping secret the execution of its victim, in this far does it abandon every claim of prevention and rests its case for punishment on vengeance and cruelty alone. The rulers of this generation, who are ashamed of their deeds, may be wiser and more sensitive than those of the last, but our ancestors, although less refined, were much more logical and infinitely more honest than are we.

The whole question of punishment is not only proven but fully admitted by our rulers in their dealings with the death penalty. It is now everywhere admitted that the brutalizing effects of public executions are beyond dispute. It was only after the completest evidence that the believers in the beneficence of punishment and violence abandoned public executions, for to abandon these was to utterly abandon the principle on which all punishment is based.

It would, of course, be impossible to prove the exact result of a public execution. Somewhere in a quiet rural community, growing out of sudden passion or some unexplained and temporary aberration, a man takes the life of his fellow man. To the shock incident to this fatal act is added a long public trial in the courts where every detail is distorted and magnified and passed from tongue to tongue until even the lisping babe is thoroughly familiar with every circumstance of the case with all its harrowing details iterated and reiterated again and again. There grows up in the public mind a bitter hatred against the unfortunate victim whose antecedents, life and motives they can in no way understand or judge. It is really believed that no one has the right to look upon this person with any feeling save that of hatred, and the least word of pity or sign of sympathy for the outcast is set down as sickly sentimentalism and the mark of mental and spiritual disease. Weeks and months, sometimes even years, elapse in the slow and unending process of the courts. The whole tragedy has been well nigh forgot, at least it no longer has any vital effect upon the community. Finally it is announced that on a certain day a public hanging will take place. Once more every detail of the tragedy is recalled to the public mind; once more each man conjures up a monster in the place of the hunted, weak, doomed victim whose act no one either fathoms or seeks to understand. A sightly spot is chosen perhaps upon the village green. For several days men are kept busy erecting a strange and ominous machine; the old men and women, the middle aged, the boys and girls, the little children, even the toddling babes, filled with curiosity watch the work and discuss every detail of the weird and fatal trap. At length the day arrives for the majesty of the law to vindicate itself. From every point of the compass comes a great throng of both sexes, all conditions and ages, each to witness the most startling event of their lives; children are there, babes in arms, and even the unborn. A rope is tied around a beam, a noose is formed of the other end, a trembling, helpless, frantic, friendless victim is led up the steps, placed on a trap, his hands and feet are bound, a black cap is pulled down to hide his face, the noose is securely fastened around his neck below his ears. The crowd watches breathless with suspense, the signal is given, the trap opens, the man falls through space, he is caught in mid-air by the rope tightening about his neck, and strangling him to death. His body heaves, his legs and arms move with violent convulsions, he swings a few minutes in mid-air before the crowd, a ghastly human pendulum moving back and forth, the mortal body of a man created in the image of God whom the state has led out and killed to show the glory and majesty of law!

The advocate of punishment is right in the belief that such a scene will produce a profound impression upon all who see or hear or know. The human being does not live who can witness such a tragedy or even know its details and not receive some impression that the rest of life cannot efface. The impression must be to harden and brutalize the heart and conscience, to destroy the finer sensibilities, to cheapen human life, to breed cruelty and malice that will bear fruit in endless ways and unknown forms. No parent who loved his child and who had any of the human sentiments that should distinguish man from the brute creation, would ever dare to trust that child to witness a scene like this. Every intelligent loving mother carrying an unborn babe would close her eyes and stop her ears and retire to the darkest corner she could find lest the unborn babe marked by the baleful scene should one day stand upon the same trembling trap with a rope about his neck.

The true morality of a community does not depend alone upon the number of men who slay their fellows. These at most are very few. The true morality depends upon every deed of kindness or malice, of love or hatred, of charity or cruelty, and the sum of these determine the real character and worth of a community. Any evil consequences that could flow from a casual killing of a human being by an irresponsible man would be like a drop of water in the sea compared with a public execution by the state.

It would probably not be possible to find a considerable number of men today who would believe that a public hanging could have any but bad results. This must be true because the knowledge of its details tends to harden, embitter and render cruel the hearts of men. Only in a less degree does the publication of all the details affect the characters and lives of men, but unless they are at least published to the world, then the example is of no effect. The state which would take life without any hope or expectation that the community would in any way be bettered could not rank even among savage tribes. Such cruelty could only be classed as total depravity.

But the effect of other punishment is no whit different save in degree from that of hanging. Cultivated, sensitive people have long since deplored the tendency of newspapers to give full and vivid accounts of crimes and their punishment, and the better and humaner class of citizens shun those journals which most magnify these details. All of this has a tendency to familiarize man with violence and force, to weaken human sensibilities, to accustom man to cruelty, to blood, to scenes of suffering and pain. What right-thinking parent would place this literature before his child and familiarize his mind with violence practiced either by the individual or the state? And yet if punishment is a deterrent, the widest publicity should be given to the story of every crime and the punishment inflicted by the state.

That men even unconsciously feel that punishment is wrong is shown by their attitude toward certain classes of society. A hangman would not be tolerated in a self-respecting body of men or women, and this has been the case for many years, in fact since men made a trade of butchering their fellow man. A professional hangman is really as much despised as any other professional murderer. A detective, jailer, policeman, constable and sheriff are not generally regarded as being subjects of envy by their fellows. Still none of these are as much responsible for their acts as the real rulers who make and execute the law. The time will come when the public prosecutor and the judge who sentences his brother to death or imprisonment will be classed with the other officers who lay violent and cruel hands upon their fellows.

If the imprisonment of men tended to awe others into obedience to law, then the old ideas of penal servitude are the only ones that can be logically sustained. A prison should be the most horrible, gruesome, painful place that can be contrived. Physical torture should be a common incident of prison life. The victim himself is beyond the pale of society. His life should be used to aid the community by the frightful example: dark dungeons, noxious smells, vermin, rats, the hardest, most constant toil, long terms of imprisonment, and the red mark to be branded on his brow, when he at last is turned loose to the light of day. Prisons should be open to the public, so that the old and young can constantly witness the terrible effects of crime. Prisons and jails should be in every community and in the most conspicuous place. The young should not be left to casually hear of public punishments or to imagine a penal institution. The living horrible example in all its loathsome, sickening details should be ever kept before their eyes. Most men now regard these public exhibitions of the malice of the state exactly as they now look on public hangings, as tending to degrade and debauch and harden the hearts of those who become familiar with the sight. But if the open sight and knowledge of a penal institution tends to degrade and harden the heart, then the secret, imperfect, covert knowledge produces the same effect only in less degree.

All communities and states are in reality ashamed of jails and penal institutions of whatever kind. Instinctively they seem to understand that these are a reflection on the state. More and more the best judgment and best conscience of men are turned toward the improvement of prisons, the introduction of sanitary appliances, the bettering of jail conditions, the modification of punishment, the treatment of convicts as men. All of this directly disproves the theory that the terrible example of punishment tends to prevent crime. All these improvements of prison conditions show that society is unconsciously ashamed of its treatment of so-called criminals; that the excuse of prevention of crime is really known to be humbug and hypocrisy, and that the real motive that causes the punishment of crime is malice and hatred and nothing else. The tendency to abrogate capital punishment, to improve prisons, to modify sentences, to pardon convicts is all in one direction. It can lead to but one inevitable result, the abolition of all judgment of man by man, the complete destruction of all prisons and the treatment of all men as if each human being was the child of the one loving Father and a part and parcel of the same infinite and mysterious life.

CHAPTER VII

CAUSE OF CRIME

If the punishment of so-called crimes tended in any way to prevent violent acts, this tendency would be manifest in some conclusive way. Whether brotherhood, love, and non-resistance would lessen crime may be a matter of debate, but that punishment does not lessen it seems to be as well established as any fact that cannot be absolutely proved. The death penalty was for years drastically enforced for the crime of smuggling, but its enforcement in no way tended to prevent the practice, which flourished in spite of executions without number,—the common consciousness would not accept this punishment as just and finally rulers were forced to modify the punishment in self-defence. The punishment of death for larceny did not prevent the crime. Nearly every religion has made its way in the face of the severest penal statutes. Its converts have all been criminals and they have accepted and taught their faith at the risk of life. Every organization of working men has grown up in violation of human laws, and the jails, prisons and scaffolds have been busily engaged in suppressing this species of crime; but in spite of the fact that judges still imprison and execute for this crime, these associations are now almost as firmly established as any institution of the world. All new political ideas, democracy, socialism, nihilism have met the same fact and have made their way regardless of scaffolds and jails. Even in the common crimes, like burglary and larceny, prisons have had no effect. From the dawn of civilization an endless procession of weak and helpless victims, handcuffed, despised and outlawed, have been marching up to prison doors, and still the procession comes and goes. Time does not stay nor punishment make it less. In fact the older the community and the better settled and undisturbed its life, the greater the number of these unfortunates whom, for some mysterious reason, the Infinite has decreed a life of shame and a death of ignominy and dishonor. If scaffolds and prisons and judges and jailers have no effect to prevent and lessen crime, common wisdom, to say nothing of humane instincts, ought to seek some other plan.

Intelligent men have long since ceased to believe in miracle or chance. Whatever they may think of ancient miracles and the original chance that brought the universe into being, still most people now believe that the world's affairs, be they small or great, physical, intellectual, or moral, come within the realm of law.

In the ordinary affairs of life, men everywhere seek the causes that produce effects. Men are called into being, live their lives, and pass away in obedience to natural laws which are as immutable as the movement of the tides. In our half civilized condition we partially comprehend this fact. The defect of the born cripple, the idiot, the insane, is no longer charged to the poor victim who, unhampered by the world, still has a burden as heavy as should be given to mortal man to bear. The physician who would treat fever or measles or diphtheria without considering the cause would be considered the veriest bungler and responsible for his patient's death. It is not so very long ago that a world about as intelligent as our own believed that disease, deformity, and sin came from the same cause,—some sort of an evil spirit that found its abode in man. The way to destroy the evil spirit was generally to destroy the man. The world will perhaps grow wise enough to not only believe that disease, deformity, and sin have a common cause, but perhaps so wise as to find their common cause. No skilful physician called to the bedside of a child suffering with scarlet fever would upbraid the child for the evil spirit that caused its pain; no more would he punish the consumptive for his hacking cough; he would understand perfectly well that the physical condition of each was due to some natural cause, and that the disease could be cured in these patients and avoided with others only when the cause was destroyed, or so well known that no one need fall a victim to the malady. Even in diseases of the most contagious sort, where the isolation of the patient is necessary to protect the lives and health of others, this isolation would be accomplished not in hatred or malice but in the greatest tenderness and love, and the isolation would last only for the purpose of a cure and a sufficient time for cure; and every pain would be taken to destroy and stamp out the cause which produced the disease.

The theory of disease is so well understood today that our physicians clearly recognize mental disease as well as physical. Insanity is no longer punished as a crime as in the days gone by, and even kleptomania is now a well classified and recognized disease. No intelligent person doubts the disease of kleptomania; its symptoms are too well established. When a person steals a thing he does not need, it is an evidence of kleptomania, an ungovernable will. When a poor person takes a thing he needs and cannot live without, there is no evidence of an ungovernable will.

Many facts have been classified concerning physical disease and our knowledge of its nature, cause, and cure grows year by year. Malignant spirits and accident are no longer considered in reference to disease; while the origin of all bodily ailments is not yet known, so many have been ascertained as to make it sure that with sufficient knowledge, all could be traced to their natural cause. And while the means have not yet been found to cure each disease, still so much is known as to warrant the belief that there is no physical ailment that will necessarily cause death.

And intelligent research is constantly adding to the known and ever narrowing the realm of the mysterious and unexplained. In physical disease, long observation has shown that certain climates and certain localities are favorable to this disease or that; some places naturally breed malaria, and the mind of man is turned to discovering methods to overcome the conditions which produce the disease. If fevers abound, the conditions are carefully observed to find what breeds the infectious germ. It is not difficult to imagine that if the medical profession should ever labor purely to cure disease, instead of to make money for itself, and should continue its research and investigation, that few would die until old age should terminate life as simply and naturally as birth ushers it in.

But in the realm of the mental and the moral, the law has been content for centuries to rest at ease. Our practical dealings with crime are based on the same theories of evil and evil spirits that made wise physicians drive the devils into swine and swine into the sea. If any progress has been made it has been in believing that, instead of one being possessed of a devil, he really is a devil. When the physical condition of a man is sufficiently far removed from the physical condition of the average which is supposed to represent the normal man, he is treated for the disease. When the mental condition sufficiently varies from that of the ordinary man, the normal man, he is promptly imprisoned or put to death. Judges and juries debate and ponder over the question of whether a man has done some act that is not commonly done by his fellows, and if they determine that he is guilty of doing the act, the judgment follows that he must have wilfully and perversely chosen to do wrong. No one then inquires why he did the act and whether there are conditions of disease present in the community that will lead others to do like acts. There is but one thing to do. The man is evil. The state must lay violent hands upon him—must meet evil with evil, violence with violence. There is but one cure for malice and that is malice.

But however ignorant the law and its administrators, some of the rules of conduct have been brought to light; while judges have been sentencing, and hangmen and jailers plying their gruesome trades, there have been thinkers and students and historians, who did not believe in the old theory of witchcraft and evil spirits on which human punishment really rests. These students and scholars have labeled and classified facts and have at least learned something as to the cause and origin of what men call crime. Enough at least has been discovered to prove that punishment has absolutely no effect to lessen crime.

The ancients believed in the existence of the body and the soul as independent entities. Each had its own sphere of action and neither one had any relation to the other. This idea has come down to us and is present in all our dealings with our fellow man. Particularly is this the view of government in its tender care of those who are the subjects of its laws. The care and treatment of the body come within the province of the physician. The care and treatment of the soul belong to the priest and the hangman. Whether man has a soul that ever existed or can exist independent of the body may be a question that will remain forever open to occupy our thoughts. But this at least is true: that the condition of the body has the greatest influence over the mental and so-called moral nature of man. The body and mind grow together and decay together. Health in one generally indicates health in the other. The overfeeding or the starvation of the one means the disease of the other. It is doubtful if any mental characteristic or abnormal condition could not be traced to its physical cause either in the individual or his ancestors, if science were far enough advanced.

Everyone who is familiar with the inmates of jails and penal institutions has learned to know the type of man that is confined as a criminal. In nearly every case these are inferior physically to the average man. In nearly every case they are also inferior mentally to the average man. One needs but visit our criminal courts day after day to find that the average criminal is a stunted, starved, deficient man. More than this, almost universally they come from the poorer class—men and women reared in squalor and misery and want, surrounded from youth by those who have been compelled to resort to almost any means for life; people who, whatever their own code of ethics, have not been able in their growth to maintain those distinctions in conduct which to the common mind constitutes the difference between lawful and unlawful acts. Here and there, of course, one finds some one in jail who has been differently reared; but these are the exceptions which in no way disprove the rule. These cases too can be traced to their cause like all the rest. There are certain moral diseases like speculation, for instance, that seize on men exactly as the measles or the mumps. These diseases generally flourish in great cities and are not indigenous to country life. Not only are these prisoners deficient in stature and intellect, but the shape of their heads shows them different from other men. As a class their heads are much less symmetrical and what are known as the higher faculties are much less developed than with the ordinary man.

If it were established even that the criminal type is inferior mentally and physically and that they have all misshapen heads, this alone ought to be sufficient to raise the inquiry as to who was responsible for their acts. Long ago a wise man said that no one could by taking thought add a cubit to his stature, and yet we hang and pen because these unfortunates have not grown as tall, as large, or as symmetrical as the ordinary man. But the mental actions of man have been shown to be as much due to law and environment as his physical health,—certain sections of the world are indigenous to men who kill their fellows; and more than this, certain portions produce men who kill with guns, others who kill with a knife, others still who administer poison. In certain sections, the chief crime is horse stealing; in others, running illicit distilleries; again, burglary; in some places, poaching; sometimes, robbery; and again, smuggling. A study of conditions would reveal why each of those crimes is indigenous to the particular soil that gives them birth, and just as draining swamps prevents the miasma, so a rational treatment of the condition caused by the various crimes would cure them, too. If our physicians were no more intelligent than our lawyers, when called to visit a miasmic patient, instead of draining the swamp they would chloroform the patient and expect thus to frighten all others from taking the disease.

Observation as to so-called crime has gone much further. The number of inmates of our jails is much larger in winter than in summer, which ought to show that there is something in the air that produces a wicked heart in the winter, or that many persons directly or indirectly go to jail because in winter, food and warmth are not easily obtained and work is hard to get. For many years it has been observed that jails are very much more crowded in hard times than in good times. If work were sufficiently plentiful or remunerative both jails and almshouses would be compelled to close their doors. Long ago it was ascertained from statistics that the number of crimes rose and fell in exact accord with the price of bread. All new communities, where land is cheap or free and labor has ample employment, or, better still, a chance to employ itself, are very free from crime. England made Australia its dumping ground for criminals for years, but these same criminals when turned upon the wide plains with a chance to get their living from the soil, became peaceable, orderly citizens fully respecting one another's rights. England, too, used certain portions of her American colonies where she sent men for her country's good. These criminals, like all the criminals of the world, were the exploited, homeless class. When they reached the new country, when they had an opportunity to live, they became as good citizens as the pilgrim fathers who were likewise criminals themselves. As civilization has swept westward through the United States, jails have lagged behind. The jail and the penitentiary are not the first institutions planted by colonists in a new country, or by pioneers in a new state. These pioneers go to work to till the soil, to cut down the forests, to dig the ore; it is only when the owning class has been established and the exploiting class grows up, that the jail and the penitentiary become fixed institutions, to be used for holding people in their place.

CHAPTER VIII

THE PROPER TREATMENT OF CRIME

Reason and judgment as well as an almost endless array of facts have proven that crime is not without its cause. In showing its cause, its cure has been made plain. If the minds and energies of men were directed toward curing crime instead of brutally assaulting the victims of society, some progress might be made.

It is often difficult to trace results, because their relations are not always direct and plain. Even in the realm of physical facts it is always easy to stray from the straight path between cause and effect. When we observe the conduct of men and seek to find its cause the problem is still more complex. Each human being is an entity made up of all that is and of all that has gone before. It may not be possible to tell from whence he obtained every quirk or peculiarity of his brain, but one thing is sure, he did not form his own skull and could have but little part in arranging the brain cells within the bone. This portion came from his father, this his mother gave, this was bequeathed by a bloody ancestor who died long generations since; but all who went before did their part, and gave their little mite to make the composite brain that drives its possessor here and there.

While the exact cause of any act may not be ascertained, still the general causes are beyond dispute. A stunted body means that either its owner or its ancestor has almost surely been starved and that want and hunger have left their traces on the brain. An inferior mind means some incapacity, disease or disadvantage, either in the individual or his ancestor, that has left him different from his fellow men. An unsymmetrical head may reach back to the early ape, and account for any possible seeming deficiency or peculiarity in the brain, which after all must be molded in the shape that the bone allows it to assume. Starved bodies can be cured by food. True, it may take more than one generation to cure them as it may have taken several to produce them, but, after all, they can be cured by food; and a rational humane world would commend itself more to thinking men and to the posterity which will judge us, by feeding these starved bodies rather than imprisoning them in pens. An inferior mind or an ill-shaped head can be reached in a generation or more by feeding the body that supports it, by treating it with tenderness, charity and kindness, rather than ruling it with hatred, bitterness and violence.

Nearly every crime could be wiped away in one generation by giving the criminal a chance. The life of a burglar, of a thief, of a prostitute, is not a bed of roses. Men and women are only driven to these lives after other means have failed. Theirs are not the simple, natural lives of children, nor of the childhood of the world; but men and women can learn these professions or be bred to them. After other resources are exhausted they will be chosen for the simple reason that life is sweet. With all its pangs and bitterness, it is the nature of life to send its poor tendrils deep into the earth and cling with all its force and power to this poor, fleeting, transitory world.

Men are slow to admit that punishment is wrong and that each human soul is the irresponsible, unconscious product of all that has gone before; and yet every kind and wise parent in the world proves by his every relation with his child that he knows that he is the author of his being and the molder of his character, and that he, the parent, is infinitely more responsible for the soul he launches than is the child himself. There might be some measure of justice in trying and punishing the parent for the conduct of the child, but even this does not reach back. The source of every life runs back to the Infinite itself. Every right thinking father does his best to have his child reared in those influences and surroundings which will best contribute to his physical, mental and moral growth. Even then he feels that the future is doubtful enough; that man is weak and finite and blind; that he sees but a little way into the dim, uncertain future; that he is filled with passions, emotions and desires; that he must travel a path beset with all sorts of temptations and promises; that his weak sight will look upon beautiful cities and fair prospects which are only mirages and sent to beguile and ensnare his soul. Few judges, if called upon, would not sooner slay their innocent sleeping child with their own loving hands, than abandon him to grow up in the streets or make his way unaided through the tangled mazes that confront the homeless and the poor; and yet these same judges will coolly arraign men who all their lives have walked in the shadows through a tangled maze beset with passion and fear, and sentence them to death and ask God to have mercy on their souls. Every man who loves his child and seeks to surround him with what is best for his physical, mental and moral needs denies in his very life the right of man to judge and punish his fellow man.

CHAPTER IX

IMPOSSIBILITY OF JUST JUDGMENT

Natural laws rule the world. It is a mistake to believe that the conduct of man is outside of natural law. The laws of being that move all the sentient world rule him. His first impulse is to preserve his life, and his next to preserve the species. Nature planted these instincts so deeply in his being that no civilization can root them up. To destroy these instincts would be to destroy the human race. The first instinct of man is to preserve his life. To do this he must obtain the food, shelter and raiment that enable him to live. His constant effort has been ever to get these at the smallest expenditure of time and strength. In a semi-coöperative state like ours the strongest choose the easiest, most remunerative occupations society can bestow. The less fortunate the next best, and so on down the scale. At the lowest place some are forced to abject toil, to practical slavery, to beggary, to crime. Men would not steal sheep if they had land on which to raise mutton. Men would not explore their neighbors houses at dead of night, if their own were filled; and women would not sell their bodies if society left them any other fairly decent and pleasant way to live.

Even if punishment by the state could ever be justified, no man is wise enough or good enough to administer that punishment. It is the theory of the law that by means of its magical wisdom it is enabled to fix a code enumerating the acts that are sufficiently evil to constitute a crime; and for each of these enumerated acts it sets a penalty which it presumes is sufficiently severe and drastic to in some mysterious way atone for, excuse, absolve, or at least in some way make right, or certainly make better, the commission of the act. Punishment must proceed upon the theory that some are wilfully bad, possessed of devils, and the bad must be punished when found bad, to prevent others who are bad from committing crime. Men could only be punished because they were wilfully bad. If men are part good and part bad it will not do to punish. How could the law or courts fix the exact line as to how bad a man might be to deserve punishment, and how good to excuse it?

Neither is it the act that should be punished, for it would be a hard and cruel and strange code of negative ethics that should say that a man should be punished for an evil act and not be rewarded for a virtuous one; and even judges might find difficulty in balancing the good and bad; and besides, does not the law in its wisdom say that an evil act shall be punished regardless of its consequences? I may steal my neighbor's horse at night and return it in the morning. I am none the less a thief and my home is the prison. I may burglarize a safe and find it empty, but the crime has been completed and it deserves the penitentiary. In each case I deserve the penitentiary because my heart is bad. Thus the old theory is the only one on which the believer in punishment could rest for a moment, that some men are bad and some are good—at least some are bad.

The law is not concerned with the good. Its business is not rewarding, but punishment; not love but hate. How can human judgment determine what heart is bad? Men's lives are a strange mixture of thought, motive and action; an infinite mixture of good and evil, as it is given to finite man to know good and evil. No life is wholly good, and no life is wholly bad. A life of great virtues may here and there be interspersed with an evil act. The law picks out the evil and ignores the good. A life barren of real affirmative goodness may still be free from serious positive sin, and thus escape the condemnation of man and his courts. The conduct which falls under the observation of others is not so much due to the goodness or badness of the heart as to the emotion or placidity of the nature. In balancing the evil of a life against the good, no one can give the exact weight to each, for no two men weigh moral worth or turpitude with the same scales. Neither can a man's standing be determined until his life is done. Acts which seem evil if left to develop character are often the means of softening the heart, of developing love and charity and humanity, of really building up the moral worth of man. But no person can be judged even by his conduct. Goodness and evil are both latent in man and this fact shows the evil of resistance and force. One may be intrinsically good and live a long life and still never be touched upon the proper side to develop character and reveal to the world the real self. It requires circumstance, opportunity and the proper appeal to develop the best in man, the same as to develop the worst in man. To judge the character of a human soul from one isolated act, would be as impossible as to judge his physical health by testing his sight or hearing alone. Every person's first impressions show how often these are really wrong, and how much they depend upon the circumstances of time and place. To really judge another's character requires almost infinite knowledge, not of their acts alone, but of their thoughts and aspirations, their temptations, and environment, and every circumstance that makes up their lives. But if the administration of punishment is to depend on the good or evil of the man, then each person must be judged from his own standpoint. One's merit or demerit depends not on what he does but on his purpose and intent, upon his desire to do good or evil. In short, upon the condition of his heart, which can only be told in part from his isolated acts.

Each person has his own rule of conduct and of life. The highest that can be done by any human soul is to live and strive according to his best conception of the highest life. To one man an act appears harmless which to another is a heinous crime. One man would blaspheme, but under no circumstances would beat a dog or kill a fly. One might commit larceny or even murder by the very strength of his love. Again, real character, merit and demerit cannot be judged except in view of the capacity, the opportunity, the teaching of the life. No honest judgment of the worth of any soul can be measured except with full knowledge of every circumstance that made his life, and with this knowledge the man who would accuse would but condemn himself. But even if every act of every life were open to the sight of man, this could furnish no guide to true character. The same temptation does not appeal alike to all. One man may not be tempted by strong drink and may never fall. Another with an appetite born in a remote ancestor may struggle manfully and fail. The temptation to take property by force does not appeal to one who can get it by inheritance or gift or fraud. The desire to kill never moves the soul of the placid man. To know what it means requires an intimate, infinite knowledge of every emotion of the soul, of every fiber of the body, and the understanding, not of how the temptations or inducements that he met would affect the judge, but how they would affect the man. Science has determined a way to measure the height and the girth of an individual, to tell the color of his eyes and hair, to determine the shape and contour of his skull. It has not yet found a way to look beneath the skull and weigh the actions and responsibilities of that hidden involved mystery—the human brain, or to look at the real man,—the human soul, and judge whether the Infinite Maker made it white or black. If every man who passed an unjust judgment on his fellow should be condemned, how many judges would be found so vain and foolish as to review and condemn their Maker's work?

CHAPTER X

THE JUDGE OF THE CRIMINAL

But even if some men deserve punishment, who is to judge? The old injunction still comes back and ever will return when man arraigns his fellow, "Let him who is without sin cast the first stone." To find a judge without sin in the ordinary meaning of the world is necessarily out of the question. They must of course pretend to be holier than the rest, and organized society helps out the farce and fraud. At the best, one guilty man is set up to judge another,—one man filled with his weaknesses, his infirmities, his shortcomings, sets himself up to judge not only that his fellow man is a criminal but that he himself is better than his fellow. And yet all the past and the present has conspired to make him good, to keep him from temptation, that he might the better pass judgment on another, while all the world has conspired to place the victim where he is. Verily, in the light of infinite justice, no greater crime could be committed than to judge and condemn your fellows and if there shall ever be a final day when the crooked is made straight and the purpose of all shall be revealed and understood, safer far will be the man who has received the sentence than the one who has dared to pass judgment on another's life and pronounce it bad.

But how is this judge to determine the guilt or innocence of his fellow? He cannot know his life and does not seek to know. To understand fully another's life would require infinite pains and such research as no judge could give or pretend to give. The judge cannot balance up the character of his victim; he simply seeks in a poor, clumsy, imperfect way to ascertain whether he did a certain act. Whatever else he did, his attitude of mind, his necessities, his early training, his opportunities and temptations, the number of temptations resisted before one proved too much—all of this is beyond the power of a human judge to know; yet all of it bears upon the real character of the man and should go to show whether, on the whole, he deserves blame or praise, and the extent of each.

In the light of all this, how many human souls could be guiltily cast out as bad? It requires infinite pains and almost infinite knowledge to judge one's physical condition. A man is suffering from some ailment and a doctor is called to treat him. The disease may be of long standing and located in some organ beyond the reach of sight and hearing; he patiently watches every symptom to know the real condition of the physical man and the cause that made him ill. He calls the wisest surgeons to consult and these may never be able to locate the disease, or the cause that made the patient as he is. But twelve untutored jurors and a judge wantonly and carelessly set themselves up to pass on the condition of a human soul—a soul no man has seen or by any chance can ever see,—a life they do not know and could not understand and do not even seek to understand. They take this soul and, with their poor light, which at the best is blackest darkness, they pronounce it bad, and in violence and malice deny it the right of fellowship with its human brothers, each equally a portion of the great Infinite which takes all of good and all of bad and makes of these one great, divine, inclusive whole.

The judge must and does view the conduct of his victim according to his own ideas of right and wrong. At his best he takes with him to the judgment tribunal every prejudice, bias and belief that his education, surroundings and heredity have left on him. He measures the condemned by the ideal man, and the ideal man must be himself, or one made from his weak, fallible concepts of right and wrong. Naturally he places little weight or value upon those vices which are a portion of his own character, or those virtues which he does not possess, or especially admire. A judge can see no character or virtue in an accused man, who would rather suffer imprisonment or death than to betray his fellows. In the judgment of the courts the betrayer is rewarded, the man of character and worth condemned. A judge reads the code, "Thou shalt not steal." He cannot understand how a so-called thief should have forcibly taken a paltry sum. He cannot conceive that he, himself, could under any circumstances have done the like. Such conduct must come from a depraved and wicked heart—a devil that dwells within the culprit. The common thief looks at the judge arrayed in fine linen and living in luxury and ease, with nothing to do but pass judgment on his fellowman. He dimly understands how much easier it is for the judge to obtain his large salary than for him to get the poor wages of his hazardous and shifting trade. But the judge does not begin to comprehend that, if he could not have received his salary or obtained a tolerable life in any of the endless grades of activity between his profession and the thief's, very easily he might have been the victim with some other fortunate man to pronounce him bad. Human judgments are not passed in view of all the circumstances of the case. If this was the condition of human judgments, no man could be condemned.

CHAPTER XI

THE MEASURE OF PUNISHMENT

But admitting the right to punish, where is there a man with the wisdom to inflict punishment? By what magical scales can he weigh the guilt of a human being, and by what standard can he determine the judgment that is proportionate to his guilt? It must be evident that the wit of man never did invent or can invent a measure that shall determine the just amount of punishment for any human act. The punishment administered does not in any way indicate the extent of the culprit's transgression, but simply shows the degree of brutality of the law, and of those who are given the power of fixing the extent of punishment to be imposed. The victim whom the law catches in its net is at the mercy of the judge. His fate depends not upon his life, not upon what society has done for him, nor upon how he has repaid the debt. Nor does it depend upon the intrinsic value of his soul, for no human judgment can reach this. Neither does it depend upon the ratio between the brain he had, and the temptation he resisted, or the ratio between the overpowering force he met and the weak will and intellect which heredity had bequeathed to him. His fate rests with the humanity or inhumanity displayed, the point of view, the experience, the prejudice, the social surroundings, the physical condition, the appetite or the breakfast of the judge, whose light and easy duty it is to pronounce judgment on the life or liberty of a fellow man.

Given the best equipment and the greatest knowledge and sense of responsibility on the part of the judge, how then will stand the case? A prisoner is arraigned for forcibly taking a pocket-book on the public street. The instinct to do the act may have come upon him in a moment's time, as the opportunity seemed suddenly present and the need seemed great. Under the peculiar circumstances of the time and place, he may have been impelled to act when a moment's reflection would have stayed his hand. In a hundred cases the opportunity for the reflection was present, and he passed through unscathed, and then there came a time when the judgment had no chance to speak and he was lost. The crime even at its worst differs only in degree, perhaps not in that, from the actions of our daily lives. We look at another's pocketbook and covet it, or covet his home or coat or wealth—the case presents the same evil heart. Our action, however, is tempered and controlled by judgment and the power of will.

Assuming the man is bad, where is the judge who can measure the punishment he ought to have? How many endless, silent, shameful days, each made of hours that seem eternities, should he be confined for this? How many days should drag their endless weary length into months and years before the act should be atoned? And is justice done when the victim, old and bent, and silent, and gray, with health destroyed and character and hope forever gone, is once more led out into the strange, bewildering light of day?

There can be no measure for human conduct. All scales, rules and measures are valueless when used to judge the soul. Even time cannot be counted. The judge upon the bench lightly consigns his victim to a prison pen. He measures the victim's years by the swiftly gliding days that pass like magic in his joyous life. To the judge, time strides with seven league boots; even the grim specter at the end, the one skeleton at his feast, even this ever-present shadow but hastens the magic flight of years. But the clock that ticks away the joyous wasted moments at the banquet hall is not the same timepiece that hangs upon the penitentiary walls. One pendulum leaps gladly back and forth; the other moves with the weight and gravity of human life, of human death, of endless agony, of unmitigated pain. Time is the most obstinate of the delusive gifts that fate bequeathes to man. When we would have her speed she moves with leaden foot. When we would have her halt she flies with magic wings.

Rulers have invented and used all sorts of punishments and constantly alternated from one to the other; each one in use seeming to be inferior to some one hitherto untried. Corporal punishment has respectively come and gone. Public floggings and private floggings, tortures, and death in various ways, have met the approval and then the disapproval of the governing power. But with all of them, crime has gone on and on, unmindful alike of the form or extent of the punishment in vogue.

The effect of an act of cruelty and violence can never be measured or understood. No one can tell the full consequences that occur to every human being when the state puts one to death, or flogs, or maims, or imprisons, or even fines. A violent act produces injury, hardship and suffering to the victim who is powerless in the strong grasp of the law. But the evil does not end with him.

In ever-widening circles the results of cruelty move on and on until to some degree or part they reach every member of society. Unless punishment lessens the sum of human suffering, increases the measure of human joy, and thus lengthens and adds to life, it has no right to be.

Punishment brings positive evil. Any possible good that it may produce is at the best problematical and wholly impossible to prove. From the first victim whom the state degrades with punishment, the evil and the hardship and suffering moves on to family and friends. In no theory of the law is compensation, or recompense, or making good, any part of punishment. If taking the life of the prisoner could bring to life the victim whom he killed there might be some apparent excuse for the punishment of death. If imprisoning in the penitentiary in any way retrieved a wrong or made up a loss, a prison might be tolerated, and some relation might be shown between punishment and crime. Even in cases where a fine is administered, in place of imprisonment, the fine does not go in any way to retrieve any loss, but goes to the state as pure punishment and nothing else. Everywhere in the theory and administration of punishment is the rule the same. The one purpose is to injure, to harm, to inflict suffering upon the individual whom society sets apart.

When traced to the end, the sole theory on which punishment is based is that a certain man has committed an act of violence and crime, and that, therefore, in some mysterious way this is to be made right by inflicting an injury on him. That the original wrong will not be undone has no bearing on the case—that others entirely innocent may suffer more grievously than the accused is not to be considered in the infliction of punishment. The father may be taken from the helpless children, and these left to grow up as best they can, with their own hardships and their father's evil name to bear, but society stands unmoved. Though the heavens fall, justice must be done, and justice can only be done by inflicting pain. The execution or imprisonment of the father may not unreasonably turn the children to follow in the path the state marked out for him. This is not the affair of government,—not prevention or recompense, or reward is the function of the state; but vengeance, vengeance sure and complete.

Justice is not the function of the state; this forms no part of the scheme of punishment. Punishment is punishment. A wife and helpless babes may be left in want when the state lays its hand in wrath upon the man. Under the law of natural justice the child has a right to support and care from the father, who is responsible for its life. Still, the state, not with a prior right, but with a greater power, takes the father from his child, kills him or pens him, and turns the child into the byways of the world, giving it only the heritage of the father's shame. It is no answer to say that such a father is of no value to the child. Many a kind, indulgent father has violated the penal codes of man. Many a father has been sent to prison because he so loved his child that he committed crime.

From the nature of things there can be no justice in punishment. Justice imposes relation between act and consequence. The judgment of man is utterly powerless to pass upon the merits or elements of a human soul. But justice from the state to its citizens imports some ratio between the rewards, opportunities and punishments meted out to each. As to rewards and opportunities, the state does nothing except to assist the strong to despoil the weak. It furnishes no opportunity for its helpless, no chance for development and life, and gives no rewards for meritorious conduct, and makes no allowance for resisting temptation from crime. But aside from all this, within the realm where the state pretends to do justice, there is no equality meted out between its various members. The code is unyielding, the positive dead letter of the law is man's highest and profoundest judgment as to the conduct of his fellows.

Each human soul is a separate entity, with its own hopes, desires, and fears; some impassive and stolid, some sensitive and shrinking. To be accused of crime means more to some natures than years of imprisonment to others. The body is not alone the subject of punishment. Man, with his tortures and cruelties, seeks to reach the mind even more than the body. Striped clothes furnish the same warmth as other garments, but to some the stripes are an ever-consuming flame. To others, properly educated and hardened by the state, this consciousness does not add to the punishment involved. One day of forced confinement, or one moment of the indignity of handcuffs, means more to some than a year of hard labor. The terms of imprisonment are not the same to all. To some a term, however short, means the blighting of a life, and the destruction of a family—perchance a wife and child, a father or a mother, whose sorrow and shame are greater for being indirect. With a sensitive soul no punishment ends when the prison gates are opened up. Its consciousness lives as long as life endures. No day is so bright, and no prospect so pleasing, but the black shadow is ever present, blighting life, and driving hope and sunshine from the soul.

In cases where fines are meted out, those who can afford to pay escape with comparative ease; others are forced to shift a burden of debt upon father, mother, wife, children, or friends, who are thus punished for years, not for crime, but for their loyalty and love. If, perchance, through any effort the money for a fine can be obtained, the state cruelly and brutally takes the unholy, ill-gotten cash, although it may mean that a home is scant of food and shivering in cold or darkness; or a little child is forced from school to a factory or store. It may mean a plundered girlhood and abandoned womanhood, that the vengeance of the state may be appeased. The taking of money by the state in payment of crime is infinitely more damnable than private theft. The evils of force and violence are unending—bold and ignorant, indeed, is he, whether ruler, official, or private citizen, who sets in motion bitterness and hate. It is an evil force set loose upon the earth to wander up and down, cankering, polluting and despoiling all it meets, augmented by every other force, to be conquered and subdued, if ever conquered and subdued, only by infinite mercy and charity and love.

Every man, whether ruler, juror, judge or whosoever that is called upon or volunteers to pass judgment on the conduct of others, must do it according to his own flickering, feeble light, according to the experiences that have made up his life. It is for this reason that good men are so bad, and bad men so good. Life ordinarily means breadth. Some, of course, are born deaf and blind, and the longer they travel the road the more contracted, cold and uncharitable they become; but to the ordinary person life means suffering and, above all other lessons, it teaches charity. As the real man grows older, less and less does he believe in or administer punishment, and more and more does he see the extenuating circumstances that explain and excuse every act. The stern and upright judge is an impossibility. No one can be stern and upright. In proportion as he becomes truly upright, really just, the more nearly he approaches the character of the ideal judge, the more nearly does he understand the injustice of violence and cruelty, and the eternal unfailing righteousness of charity and love. Where is the man so wise or the judge so great and just that he could take any two human beings with their different ancestry, environment, opportunities, passions and temptations, and pronounce a judgment that would equalize the two?

Lawmakers, since the world began, have been busy undoing each other's wrongs. Courts have been established whose sole duty it is to correct other courts. Unjust judgments are necessarily incident to the infirmities of man. The wise judge who looks back over a long career, the judge who knows human life and has a human heart, the judge who seeks to be ruled by his conscience, will find much in his past career he would wish undone. He will look back on many unjust judgments, on many things done in anger and hatred, cruelty and wrong, on blighted hopes and ruined lives. But in his whole career he will regret no act of charity, no deed of mercy that he has been moved to do. He will look back on judgments he would reverse, but these are not judgments of love or forgiveness or charity, but judgments of force, of violence, of hate.

CHAPTER XII

WHO DESERVES PUNISHMENT

If there is any justice in human punishment it must be based upon the theory of intrinsic evil in the victim. Punishment cannot be justified because of the violation of human law. To violate law is often the highest, most sacred duty that can devolve upon the citizen, and even were it not, the condition of the heart is the test of the evil or good purpose, not the good or evil of the act. The world worships and venerates many of its dead because they violated human law. Every new religion, every social advancement has been carried on in violation of human law. The criminals who, in the face of contumely, hatred or violence, have led the world to a higher standard and brought humanity to a diviner order, have so loved truth and righteousness as to defy the law, and in every age these men have met the life of outcasts, and the death of felons. Whatever may be said of the necessity of government to protect itself, no one can believe that any human being merits punishment for following his own highest ideal. Punishment can only be in any wise defended upon the theory that the individual is untrue to himself, that his heart is bad. But all schemes of human punishment seem specially contrived to exempt this class of men. Those who are untrue to themselves find no difficulty in obeying the state, or at least in seeming to be subservient to its laws. The cunning man without strong convictions of right and wrong can always find ample room to operate his trade inside the dead line the law lays down. Even Blackstone wrote that a man who governed his conduct solely by the law was neither an honest man nor a good citizen. The penal code cannot pretend to cover all the vicious acts of men. If there is a distinction between vicious acts and righteous acts, each are so numerous that even to catalogue them would be beyond the power of the state. The most that the penal code pretends to do is to choose a number of fairly well classified acts and to set penalties for these crimes. The men who really entail the most evil and suffering on mankind easily shape their conduct to avoid these acts. If perchance they wish in effect to do some things forbidden by the law, they are able by their wealth to have skilled lawyers who can show them how to accomplish the same object by indirect means. The hollow hearted man, the whited sepulcher is the last to violate the law. To support the state and be noisily patriotic is a large part of his stock in trade. As a rule it is only the weak or the extremely conscientious or devoted that violate the law, and it does not follow that these or any other class really intend a wrong or consider it in any such light as their judge, when they commit an act forbidden by the law.

A very large number of acts of individual violence come from sudden feeling and passion, which is purely a physical, or more properly, a mechanical act. Certain motives or feelings operating upon a given brain produce a given result; whereas operating upon another brain, they might produce a very different effect. It is like a body in mechanics operating upon another smaller or larger body. The laws of the universe are not at work in one place and held in abeyance in another. In these cases reason and judgment have no opportunity to act. Reflection and conscience in no wise enter into the affair. Feeling, emotion, passion alone are responsible for the deed. The human feelings as they sweep through that uncharted land, the human soul, produce infinitely varied results, like the moving wind, whose sound depends entirely upon the unconscious instrument with which it toys.

CHAPTER XIII

NATURAL LAW AND CONDUCT

Many of the crimes fixed by law are purely arbitrary. To commit them or to refrain does not necessarily imply innocence or guilt. Of such a character, for instance, are revenue laws, the observance of holy days and the like. A large number of forbidden acts that are generally supposed to imply moral guilt are also purely arbitrary. Most of the laws governing the taking and obtaining of property, which constitute the great burden of our penal code, are arbitrary acts, whose sole purpose is to keep the great mass of property in the hands of the rulers and exploiters and to send to jail those who help themselves and who have no other means within their power to sustain their lives. Most of the so-called thieves and other offenders against property dimly know this fact. Without being able to analyze or logically realize it, they, after all, feel that they have committed no wrong, and that they took the only road life had left open for their feet.

Nearly our whole criminal code is made up of what may be called property crimes, or crimes against property, if they may be so called. These crimes are burglary, larceny, obtaining property by false pretenses, extortion, and the like. The jails and penitentiaries of every nation in the world are filled to overflowing with men and women who have been charged with committing crimes against property. Probably nine-tenths of all the business of criminal courts come directly from property crimes. A very large proportion of the balance comes indirectly from this cause. Nothing could more completely show the humbuggery, knavery and the absolute hypocrisy of all punishment by the state than the patent facts with reference to these crimes. From first to last these inmates of jail and penitentiary, these suffering outcast men, are utterly without property and have ever been. In the penal institutions of the world are confined a motley throng charged with committing assaults upon property, and yet this whole mass of despised and outcast humanity have ever been the propertyless class, have never had aught whereon to lay their heads. But where is all the property that has been the subject of these dire assaults? No matter where you turn your eyes in the world, the whole property is in the hands of a chosen few, and the so-called owners of all this wealth created by the labor of man and the bounty of nature—these so-called owners have committed no crime against property. The statement of the fact is sufficient to show the inequality of the whole system under which the fruits of the earth are kept in the possession of the few. These despised and outcast ones have violated no law of conscience or justice, have committed no unrighteous assault on property. The plain fact that will one day stand clearly forth to explain the whole brutal code which is used to imprison and enslave,—the plain reason and object of these laws is the fact that the rulers who have forcibly seized the earth have made certain rules and regulations to keep possession of the treasures of the world, and when the disinherited have reached out to obtain the means of life, they have been met with these arbitrary rules and lodged in jail.

The advocates of punishment believe that law controls the natural world. The movement of the earth about the sun, the changes of the moon, the rising and falling of the tide, the change of seasons, all these depend on natural law. It is even known that the distribution of animal life upon the earth is due to natural law. Certain climates and locations produce certain animal life. Particular seasons of the year increase or diminish insect life. The wild fowl flies north in summer and south in winter. The swarming of bees, the homes of ants, in short all the activities, lives and deaths of the brute creation are surely seen to be the subject of natural law. The distribution, growth and decay of plant life is no less within the realm of law than is the animal life, which depends upon the same powers and forces, the same great source of life.

But when man is reached it would seem that the rule of law is at an end. His life and death, his goings in and out, his myriad acts are due to no rule or system or law, but are the result of capricious will alone. True, in many of his acts man recognizes the great force in whose mighty power he is like the insect, or the grain of sand tossed by the angry sea. Here and there he seems to dimly understand the great laws of necessity, of sequence, of consequence, that govern human life. Every father who takes pains in the rearing of his child, who surrounds it with the influences that build up character and develop judgment and reason, recognizes the law of necessity, the controlling power of environment, the strength of habit and circumstance. The life of tribes and races and nations show that fixed laws control in the actions of men, as everywhere else within the realm of nature. Man is a part of nature, the highest evolution of all, but still a part firmly bound by law to every atom of matter and every particle of force which the wide universe contains. The life and death of man, his distribution over the earth, his permanency as an individual or a tribe, depend upon all other life. Man draws his sustenance from the animate and inanimate world. The lives of bees depend upon the flowers, their number and condition, their coming and going; their birth and death is due to this natural cause outside the control of the individual bee. The life of man depends upon his supply of food and shelter, upon his ability to obtain the necessities of life. It is true that in his progress he is no longer bound so closely to the earth as in his early stages. He has learned something of the laws of nature and is able to take some thought for the morrow; but yet famine destroys him, disease overcomes him; severe droughts, protracted heat, great inundations of flood, all these affect his life, change population, destroy vast numbers, always the weaker, those less able to provide for themselves, those who, from circumstances, have taken the smallest thought for the morrow.

Even in the most civilized, progressive lands man is dependent on nature. The constant thought of much the largest portion of mankind is for the procurement of those things that will sustain, prolong and render their lives more comfortable. The vast majority of men are closely bound to the soil and their whole life is a struggle for the means to live. Even the large majority of those whose condition is the most tolerable find life an endless struggle and anxiety their constant companion. Such a thing as a free choice of life is out of the question for the vast majority of men born upon the earth; their residence, occupation, hours of labor, method of life, are fixed almost irrevocably in obedience to the demands of their physical being. After those whose conditions of life are the most tolerable come a great mass whose existence is most precarious, dependent upon the condition of the harvest, the condition of trade, the amount of rain or snow, the quantity of sunshine, and a thousand circumstances far beyond their control.

As a consequence of his desire for life and the means that make it certain and pleasant, man has ever turned his attention toward the conquest of nature, reducing vegetable and animal life to his control. But his conquest does not end here. Not vegetables and animals alone must be his slaves, but man as well. Ever has man enslaved his fellow; from the beginning of his career upon the earth he has sought to make his own existence pleasanter and more certain by compelling others to toil for him. In its more primitive stages slavery was enforced by the ownership of the man. In its later and more refined stages it is carried on by the ownership of the things from which man must live. All life comes primarily from the earth and without access to this great first source of being, man must die. Passing from the ownership of individuals, rulers have found it easier and more certain to own the earth—for to own the earth is to fix the terms on which all must live. More and more does the master seek to control access to land, to coal, to timber, to iron, to water—these prime requisites to life. More and more certainly, as time and civilization move on, do these prime necessities pass to the few. Every new engine of production makes it easier for the few to reduce the earth to their possession. Even land itself is of no value without the railroads, the harbors, the mines and the forest. Everywhere these have passed into the hands of the few. From the private ownership of men, the rulers have passed to the private ownership of the earth and the control of the land. The rulers no longer have the right to buy and sell the man, to send him here and there to suit their will. They simply have the power to dictate the terms upon which he can stand upon the earth. With the mines, the forests, the oil, the harbors, the railroads, and the really valuable productive land in the rulers' hands, the dominance and power of man over his fellows is absolute and complete. It is not necessary to show that it is the ruling class who own the earth—the owners of the earth must be the ruling class.

CHAPTER XIV

RULES GOVERNING PENAL CODES AND THEIR VICTIMS

The rulers make penal codes for the regulation and control of the earth and all the property thereon—the earth which was made long ages before they were evolved, and will still remain ages after they are dust. Not only do they make these rules to control the earth for their brief, haughty lives, but they provide that it may pass from hand to hand forever. The generations now living, or rather those that are dead and gone, fixed the status of unborn millions, and decreed that they shall have no place to live except upon such terms as may be dictated by those who then controlled the earth. To retain all the means of life in the hands of the few and compel the many to do service to support these few requires the machinery of the state. It is for this that penal laws are made, and the effort of the despoiled to reach out in their despair and obtain a small portion of the natural heritage of all is directly and indirectly the basis of all property assaults.

Every person who has observed cattle knows that if the pasture is good the animals are quiet, and will stay where they are placed; but let the pasture grow thin until hunger comes and they will learn to jump. There were never cattle so quiet and well behaved that they could not be made to jump, and never cattle so breachy that they could not be made tame. Even successive generations of starving and abuse will not so far pervert their nature but that successive generations of kind treatment will bring them back to a peaceful, gentle life. Human beings are like cattle in a field. They are cattle in a field. Give them a chance to live and prosper, and violent acts will be unknown; but bring them close to the line of starvation or want and their natural rights assert themselves above the forms and laws that man has made to hold the earth and enslave his fellows. Of course here and there may be found cases where generations of outlawry and exploitation have left their marks upon men, until they seem to prefer this life; but in those cases fair treatment would generally remove this in the first generation, and always before many generations had come and gone.

All energy manifests itself along lines of least resistance, and the first energies of man are devoted to the procurement of the means of life. It is only where organized tyranny has made violence and force the line of least resistance that men will deviate from the normal path, and so long as the cupidity and brutal selfishness of man shall make this the line of least resistance, all the laws on earth cannot overcome the primal instincts and feelings upon which life depends. A race that would starve, or beg, or accept alms before violating the brutal laws that fence the children of nature from their source of life, would quickly degenerate into abject slavery and finally into nothingness. All so-called criminals do not reason out the cause that placed them where they are. Instinctively they feel that they are doing what they must. This class have generally lived for years, sometimes for generations, so near the border line, have lived such precarious lives that their callings and avocations have grown as natural and normal as monopolizing the earth has grown to another class. They are fully aware of the dangers incident to their craft, of the scanty recompense that their lives afford, and, like all other men, would at once abandon their calling for an opportunity to lead more normal lives. They are in no sense devoid of these common instincts of humanity upon which nature rests all life. Given a child falling into a river, an old person in a burning building, a woman fainting in the street, and a band of convicts would risk their lives to give aid as quickly at least as a band of millionaires.

Nature takes little account of atoms, her operations are on a wide field, a broad scale. She brings famine, a million men must die; she does not seem to pick out the individual men—she draws a straight hard line, and those who step across cannot return. Nature and man combine to make hard the condition of human life for the great majority that live upon the earth. A very few choose the roads of luxury and ease; the vast mass are scattered in all the avenues of life; some serve by abject toil; some enter the hazardous callings of the railroads and the mines; some the extra-hazardous of making gunpowder and nitroglycerine; and some the still more hazardous—these are thieves or burglars or robbers or prostitutes, as the case may be. Conditions improve, and man moves up in the scale; the toilers have greater luxury; those in hazardous callings take an easier place; the extra-hazardous rise to the hazardous; and the still-more-hazardous to the extra-hazardous. The conditions of life become more severe and the current flows the other way. It is then that the jails and the penitentiaries are crowded to the utmost limit they will hold.

Statistics have shown that the number of inmates in our prisons increases with every rise in the price of food. If a combination increases the price of flour a cent a pound and ten thousand men are sent to jail throughout the world, in the judgment of infinite wisdom and justice who will be held responsible for the crime? Every time that the trust raises the price of coal some poor victims are sent to jail, and at every raise in the price of oil some girls are sent out upon the streets to get their bread by a life of wretchedness and shame.

That these property laws are purely arbitrary is shown by the slightest thought. The criminal statutes forbid extortion and swindling, and yet the largest part of business is extortion, and much of the balance is swindling. When the law forbids extortion and swindling, it simply forbids certain forms and methods of these acts, and these forms and methods are the ones not practiced by the ruling class. They are so small and insignificant as not to constitute business but only petty annoyance to the ruling class. To go directly to a victim and by threats of violence compel him to pay more for some commodity than it is really worth is generally extortion, but this is a very clumsy and infrequent act. Real extortion is taking for any service more than it is fairly worth by means of agencies created by the extorter to despoil his victim, and this is the business of the business world. Nearly every street-car line and every gas plant in the world operates its business by means of special privileges, and from one-half to three-fourths of the money they receive is extorted from that portion of the community that has no redress. The railroad companies, who, through watered stocks and bonds and combinations, charge the consumer twice and more the value of the service given, touch the pocket of everyone who lives in a modern state. The production of iron, clothing, many kinds of food, in fact the largest part of what is used in daily life, is controlled by combinations whose sole purpose is extortion; they scheme to absolutely control the market and take from the consumers what they have. And yet for this extortion which reaches every home and despoils every fireside, the law furnishes no redress. Either it does not come within the provisions of the law or else those who are charged with its enforcement do not care to reach this sort of extortion which is the only kind that really affects the world. In either case it shows that the penal code is made and enforced by the ruling class, not upon themselves, but to keep the weak at the bottom of the social scale.

The law forbids swindling at least in certain ways, and yet a large part of business consists in making the public believe that they are getting more value for what they give than the tradesman can possibly afford. The daily papers are filled to overflowing with lying advertisements, each contradicting the other. Our fences, rocks and buildings are defaced with vulgar, hideous lies in order to swindle men out of their much-coveted cash. All our merchants and tradesmen frantically call out their lies in every form, that they may sell their wares for a larger price than they are really worth. And yet, to all of this, the criminal code has no word to say. This is not the class of swindlers it was made to reach. The man who can buy the space of a great paper to tell the wondrous qualities of the wares he has to sell is not the sort of man to come within the meshes of the penal code.

People in the jail and people out, when reproached for certain conduct, almost invariably respond that they have done no worse than someone else who stands uncondemned, and this retort is true when motives are fully analyzed and conduct thoroughly understood. The actions of men are wondrously alike. When we look at the criminal in the jail, or at our enemy in the street, we do not see the man. This is not due to him. It comes from the malice, the hatred, the want of human charity that dwells in our own hearts. Through this fog and mist there can be no clear true sight. "To the pure all things are pure." To the just all souls are really white.

The web of the law reaches so far that there are very few who have not in some way been touched by its meshes. One infallible proof as to the real nature of crime and the character of the criminal is open to almost everyone who wishes to observe. Few men are so poor and outcast as to have no friends. The victims who cluster around the corridors and entrances of our jails are as pitiable as those who dwell inside. To those friends who know him the criminal is a man, a man for whom they will sacrifice time, money, sometimes honor and even life. If it is nothing but a poor wife, or a helpless child who has known the kind heart of a husband or a father, these are there to prove that the wretch is not a monster, but a man—these are the ones who knew him, who saw his life, who touched him on the human side, the side that shows the real true kinship of man. Judges, lawyers, clergymen, physicians, all classes of men readily come forward and tell of the virtues of the criminal whom they know, they tell of the extenuating circumstances that led to his act, or they show that, in spite of these, they understand the worth of the man. The criminal is always the man we do not know or the man we hate—the man we see through the bitterness of our hearts. Let one but really love his fellow and he knows full well that he is not a criminal. He sees his pulsing heart, he knows his weak flesh, his aspiring soul, his hopes, his struggles, his disappointments, his triumphs and his failings, and he loves the man for all of these.

CHAPTER XV

THE MACHINERY OF JUSTICE

The state furnishes no machinery for arriving at justice. Even if it were possible under any circumstances to judge, and even though men were really criminals, the state has no way of arriving at the facts. If the state pretends to administer justice this should be its highest concern. It should not be interested in convicting men or punishing crime, but administering justice between men. It is obvious to the most casual observer that the state furnishes no machinery to accomplish this result. The penal law simply takes a man into its hopper and grinds out a criminal at the end. A force of able-bodied, well fed, well paid men are kept busy in their search for crime. These find pecuniary reward in the crime of their fellows. An indictment is easily returned against a friendless man—a suspicion is enough in any case where the victim has no friends. If he is poor he is at once lodged in jail. Later he is placed on trial in the courts. When he steps into the dock both judge and jurors look on him as a guilty man—believe he has committed crime. He is carefully guarded by officers, like a guilty, hunted thing. Arrayed against him is an able prosecutor, well paid, and having personal and political ambitions dependent on the number of men he grinds into criminals. The prosecutor has ample means for the conduct of the case. The prisoner, helpless enough at best, is rendered absolutely powerless to prepare his case by being lodged in jail. Without money he has no advocate with either the learning, influence, or ability to help his cause. If he is silent he is convicted. If he speaks no one believes his words. Innocent or guilty, it is a miracle if he escapes, and in this miracle the fact of his innocence or guilt plays but the smallest part. Given a few suspicious circumstances, a helpless prisoner, an indictment, and another victim is the sure result. And in the hands of a shrewd lawyer or under the belief of guilt, any circumstances are suspicious circumstances. Almost all acts are subject to various interpretations, and the guilt or innocence of a circumstance depends not upon the act but upon the mind that passes judgment on the act. We look back with horror at the criminal courts of England, of Spain, of Italy, even upon our own Puritan judges who sentenced witches to death. These judges were doubtless as intelligent as our own. Their brutal, cruel judgments did not grow from a wicked perverted heart, but from the fact that they were passing judgment on their fellow man. These unjust judgments are the fruit of the cruel system of force and barbarism which clothes one man with the authority and power to condemn his fellow. All prosecutions are malicious, and all judgments are meted out in anger and hatred. Our own judges are constantly showing this. In nearly every instance they condemn a prisoner to a term of servitude, and when passion has fled and the sane and holy feelings of mercy, of charity, of humanity once more regain their sway, they call on the pardoning power to rescind their cruel acts. In all these cases of pardons reflection shows the judges that the punishment meted out was at least too severe. The difference is in the frame of mind of the judge when engaged in the business of administering judgment, and when in the mood for listening to those feelings of human charity which are the diviner part of man.

Punishment, to in any way be justified, should diminish the sum of human misery, the result of the bitterness and hatred of men. But here, as everywhere else, punishment falls short. Wherever the judgment of courts enters it is to corrupt and to destroy. The misery and suffering entailed on man by scaffolds, racks, blocks, dungeons and jails has never yet begun to be told. Blood and misery and degradation has marked the administration of punishment

Since man first penned his fellow men,

Like brutes, within an iron pen.

Let any reasoning being consider the tens of thousands who have been burned, and hanged, and boiled, and otherwise put to death for witchcraft; the millions for heresy; the thousands of noble victims who have suffered for treason; the victims of fire, of torture, of scaffold, of rack and of dungeon, for all the conceivable crimes since time began. Let him consider the oceans of blood and rivers of tears shed by the force and brutality of the rulers of the world; the cruelty, torture and suffering heaped upon the helpless, the weak, the unfortunate; and then ask himself if he believes that punishment is good. Even could violence ever prevent crime, the brutality, suffering, blood and crime of the rulers has towered mountain high above that of the weak and obscure victims whose wrongs they have pretended to avenge. And this cruelty does not abate. It is simple madness that doubts the justice of past condemnations and believes in the righteous judgments of today. No condemnation is just, and no judgment is righteous. All violence and force are cruel, unjust and barbarous, and cannot be sustained by the judgment of men.

But the evil of judgment and punishment does not end with the unfortunate victim. It brutalizes and makes inhuman all who are touched with its power. Under the influence of punishments, jailers, policemen, sheriffs, detectives, and all who deal with prisons are brutalized and hardened. The iniquities produced upon helpless prisoners leave their effects upon the captor as well as the captives. To witness the constant suffering and indignities of prison life is to destroy the finer sensibilities of the soul. Men who are otherwise kind in the various relations of life do not hesitate at cruelty to these despised prisoners whom the law has placed outside its ban. To underfeed and overwork, to insult, degrade and beat are common incidents of prison life, and this, too, not because jailers are naturally cruel and bad, but because prisons are prisons, and convicts are outcasts. Instead of approaching these unfortunates as brothers in fellowship and love, their only concern is to make them feel that the heavy hand of the state has been laid upon them in malice and violence.

However thoroughly the futility, cruelty and injustice of punishment may be shown, men will still persist that it must exist. The thought that society could live without prisons and policemen seems to be beyond the conception of the common man. If punishment has no effect to diminish or prevent crime, then no danger would be incurred to dismiss our jailers and jurors and close our prison doors. The results of this policy can, of course, not be proven absolutely in advance, but so sure as the existence of man is consistent with justice, charity and love, so sure is this policy right and would produce good results. It is not necessary to prove the theory of non-resistance to show that this policy is practical today. Society, as now organized, rests upon violence and wrong. The non-resistant pleads for a better order, one in which the law of love and mercy will be the foundation of every relationship of man with man. The present unjust system is supported by violence and force. The unjust possessions of the rich are kept in their place by soldiers, guns and policemen's clubs. If these were withdrawn would the weak at once take the earth and all its fullness from those who for ages have ruled the world?

No violent and forcible readjustment of this sort could come. Force is wrong both to commit and to redress evil. In the rule of force the weak must always fall. For the poor and oppressed to advocate the use of force means that they must still be the victims, for the strongest force must win. All that can help the weak is the rule of brotherhood, of love. Unless this can be proved there is no way to destroy the injustice that is everywhere the rule of life. To make the weak strong, and the strong weak, could neither destroy injustice nor permanently change the wretched order of the world. A bayonet in the hand of one man is no better than in the hand of another. It is the bayonet that is evil and all of its fruits are bad.

The world must learn that violence is wrong. Individuals who understand this truth must take no part in violent acts, whether to enslave or to free. The inherent cohering forces will hold society together and cause man to cooperate for his highest good. A large part of present society is purely voluntary and due to natural law. It is for force and violence and injustice that the aid of the state is called. Society should not punish. The great burden that rests upon production to support armies, courts, and prisons, with all their endless officers and staggering weight should be taken from the shoulders of the poor. This of itself would so relieve industry and add to the possibilities of life that the very hazardous occupations that we call criminal would almost wholly disappear. The class from which these victims come is known to be the outcast and the poor. A small fraction of the vast sum squandered for violence and force would easily place all these dangerous persons beyond the temptations of criminal activity. Even now, with all the injustice of today, the expenditure of public money to relieve suffering, to furnish remunerative employment, to rationally prevent crime by leaving men with something else to do, would produce better results than all the imagined benefits that follow in the wake of scaffolds and of jails.

The effort of the penal codes has never been to reach any human being before violence is done, except to awe him by the brief transitory show of force; but after the act is done the state must spend its strength and substance for revenge. Most men are driven to criminal acts from the necessities of life and the hatred bred by the organized force they meet. Remove dire poverty, as could be easily done with a tithe of what is now spent on force; let organized society meet the individual, not with force, but with helpfulness and love; and the inducement to commit crime could not exist. Let society be the friend not the tyrant, the brother not the jailer, and the feeling will be returned a thousandfold. No man or no society ever induced love with clubs and guns. The emblem of the state is the soldier, the policeman, the court, the jail. It is an emblem that does not appeal to the higher sentiments of man—an emblem that so long as it exists will prevent true brotherhood and be a hindrance to the higher sentiments that will one day rule the world.

Even if now and then passion and feeling should gain control of man, this passion and feeling would be brief and transitory; if it accomplished destruction, no power could make it whole. The concern of society would then be to call back this soul to saner thoughts and a truer, nobler life; not to blacken and destroy, nor to plant bitter hatred and despair in the soul of one who might be brought to a fine and high realization of human conduct and human life. Under this sort of treatment a large proportion of those who commit violent deeds would be brought to a full realization of their acts, and they themselves would seek in every way to repair the ill effects of their evil deeds.

CHAPTER XVI

THE RIGHT TREATMENT OF VIOLENCE

Sentimental and humane thoughts and purposes are often, perhaps generally, based on real life, and have a natural reason for their being. To "turn the other cheek" or to "resist not evil" may seem at first glance to have no support in the facts of life, but after all that which makes for a higher humanity, a longer life, and a more vigorous community, is the true philosophy. To use violence and force upon the vicious and the weak must produce the evil that it gives. Like produces like. Clubs, jails, harsh language, brutal force, inevitably tend to reproduce the same state of mind in the victim of the assault. This is not merely a fact in human nature. It is a fact in all nature, plant and animal and man. So long as the gentle springtime rather than the cruel winter brings vegetable and animal life to an awakening earth, just so long will kindness and love triumph, produce joy and life, where force and violence bring only evil and death. Harsh treatment kills plant life, and kind treatment builds it up. Violence and brutality produce their like in animal life, and kindness tames and subdues. With gentleness and kindness a swarm of wild bees may be handled and controlled, but approach them with violence and force and each bee is converted into a criminal whose only purpose is to destroy.

With all animal life the same rule exists; even those beasts whose nature calls for a diet of flesh and blood may be subdued in time by gentleness and love. Man with his higher intellect and better developed moral being is much more susceptible to kindness and love. Likewise he more easily learns to fear and hate. Man readily discerns the feelings and judgment of his fellows, and as readily renders judgment in return. The outcast and abandoned form not the slightest exception to the rule—they know and understand the ones who meet them with gentleness and love; for these they make sacrifices, to these they are faithful, to these they exhibit the higher qualities that show the possibilities of the soul. Cases where one convicted of crime comes from a place of safety and risks his liberty and life to help save his friend are not rare in

70

the least. True comradeship and loyalty is met quite as often here as in the higher walks of life. Nothing is more common in ordinary selfish society than to see one man refuse all aid and help to another in financial need. Many convicts and outcasts could teach a much needed lesson of loyalty and generosity to the exemplary man.

No amount of treatment can reclaim an evil heart if the treatment is administered without love. As children at school we knew with our young natural instincts the teacher who loved us and the teacher who despised us—the one awoke feelings of love and kindness, the other hatred and revenge. No heart is so pure that it may not be defiled and hardened by cruelty, hatred and force, and none so defiled that it may not be touched and changed by gentleness and love. Unless this philosophy of life is true the whole teaching of the world has been a delusion and a snare. Unless love and kindness tends to love, then hatred and violence and force should be substituted and taught as the cardinal virtues of human life. The mistake and evil of society is in assuming that love is the rule of life, and at the same time that large classes of people are entirely outside its pale. No parent ever teaches his child any other philosophy than that of love. Even to quarrelsome playmates they are taught not to return blows and harsh language, but to meet force with kindness and with love. The parent who did not depend on love to influence and mold the character of the child rather than force would be regarded not as a real parent but a brute. Force is worse than useless in developing the conduct of the child. It is true that by means of force the little child may be awed by superior brute power, but he gives way only under protest, and the violence that he suppresses in his hand or tongue finds refuge in his heart. Violent acts are not evil—they are a manifestation of evil. Good conduct is not goodness. It is but a manifestation of goodness. Evil and goodness can only be conditions of the inmost life, and human conduct, while it generally reflects this inmost life, may be so controlled as not to manifest the real soul that makes the man.

Every child needs development, needs training to fit him to live in peace and right relations with his fellow man. Every intelligent and right-thinking person knows that this development must be through love, not through violence and force. The parent who would teach his child to be kind to animals, not to ruthlessly kill and maim, would not teach this gentleness with a club. The intelligent parent would not use a whip to teach a child not to beat a dog. The child is not made into the good citizen, the righteous man, by pointing out that certain conduct will lead to punishment, to the jail or the gallows. The beneficence of fear was once considered a prime necessity in the rearing of the child, and this theory peopled the earth with monsters and the air with spooks ready to reach down and take the helpless child when he wandered from the straight and narrow path; but this method of rearing children does not appeal to the judgment and humanity of today. The conduct of children can only be reached for good by pointing to the evil results of hatred, of inharmony, of force; by appealing to the higher and nobler sentiments which, if once reached, are ever present, influencing and controlling life. The code of hatred, of violence and force, too, is a negative code. The child is given a list of the things he must not do, exactly as the man is furnished a list of the acts forbidden by the state. At the best, when the limits of this list are reached and the forbidden things are left undone, nothing more is expected or demanded. But no code is long enough to make up the myriad acts of life. Kindness or unkindness can result in a thousand ways in every human relationship. If the child or the man observes the written code through fear, the unwritten moral code, infinitely longer and more delicate, will be broken in its almost every line. But if the child or the man is taught his right relations to the world and feels the love and sympathy due his fellow man, he has no need of written codes; his acts, so far as those of mortals can be, will be consistent with the life and happiness of his fellow man. And this not through fear, but because he bears the highest attitude toward life.

With our long heredity and our imperfect environment, even if the organized force of the state should disappear, even if the jails and penitentiaries should close their doors, force would only completely die in course of time. Evil environment and heredity may have so marked and scarred some men that kindness and love could never reach their souls. It might take generations to stamp out hatred or destroy the ill effects of life; but order and kindness most surely would result, because nature demands order and tolerance, and without it man must die. No doubt here and there these so-called evil ones would arouse evil and hatred in return, and some sudden act of violence would for a time occasionally be met with violence through mob law in return. But uncertain and reprehensible as mob law has ever been it is still much more excusable and more certain than the organized force of society operating through the criminal courts. Mob law has the excuse of passion, of provocation, not the criminal nature of deliberation, coldness and settled hate. Mob law, too, generally reaches the object of its wrath, while evidence is fresh and facts are easily understood and unhampered by those rules and technical forms which ensnare the weak and protect the strong. And unjust and unwise as the verdicts of mob law often are, they are still more excusable, quicker, more certain and less erring than the judgments of the criminal courts.

But neither civil law nor mob law is at all necessary for the protection of individuals. Men are not protected because of their strength or their ability to fight. In the present general distribution of weapons, in one sense, every man's life is dependent on each person that he meets. If the instinct was to kill, society as organized presents no obstacle to that instinct. When casual violence results it is not the weakest or most defenceless who are the victims of the casual violence of individuals. Even the boy at school scorns to war upon a weaker mate. The old, the young, the feeble, children and women, are especially exempt from violent deeds. This is because their condition does not call for feelings of violence, but rather awakens feelings of compassion, and calls for aid and help. The non-resistant ever appeals to the courageous and the manly. Without weapons of any kind, with the known determination to give no violence in return, it would be very rare that men would not be safe from disorganized violence. It is only the state that ever lays its hands in anger on the non-resistant.

Neither would non-resistance in the state or individual indicate cowardice or weakness or lack of vital force. The ability and inclination to use physical strength is no indication of bravery or tenacity to life. The greatest cowards are often the greatest bullies. Nothing is cheaper and more common than physical bravery. In the lower animals it is more pronounced than in man. The bulldog and the fighting cock are quite as conspicuous examples of physical bravery as the prize-fighter or the soldier. The history of all warfare shows either that physical bravery is not an indication of great excellence or that supreme excellence is very common, in fact almost a universal possession. Under the intoxication of patriotism, or the desire for glory, or the fear of contempt, most men will march with apparent willingness into the face of the greatest danger. Often it requires vastly more courage to stay at home than to enlist—more courage to retreat than to fight. Common experience shows how much rarer is moral courage than physical bravery. A thousand men will march to the mouth of the cannon where one man will dare espouse an unpopular cause. An army well-equipped and ready for action has less terror for the ordinary man than the unfavorable comment of the daily press. True courage and manhood come from the consciousness of the right attitude toward the world, the faith in one's own purpose, and the sufficiency of one's own approval as a justification for one's own acts. This attitude is not that of the coward, for cowardice is really disapproval of self, a consciousness of one's own littleness and unworthiness in the light of one's own soul, which cannot be deceived.

Intelligent men are willing to accept many truths that they believe are not fitted for the universal acceptance of mankind, and however they may feel that punishment is wrong they still urge that it will not do to teach this doctrine to the great mass of men and to carry its practice into daily life. But sooner or later all conduct and all life must rest on truth. It is only fact that can form a basis for permanent theories that tend to the preservation of the race. No one is too poor, or too young, or too vicious to know the truth, for the truth alone is consistent with all the facts of life, and this alone can furnish any rule of life. The truth alone can make free. When society is taught the truth that it is wrong to punish, to use force, to pass judgment on man, it will have no need for jails. The man who really knows and understands this truth can have no malice in his heart, can use no force and violence against his fellow, but will reach him with love and pity. The man or society that understands this truth will know that so-called crime is only so-called crime; that human conduct is what the necessities of life make of the individual soul. Then in reality, as now only partially, men will turn their attention to the causes that make crime. Then will they seek to prevent and cure, not to punish and destroy. Then man will learn to know that the cause of crime is the unjust condition of human life; that penal laws are made to protect earth's possessions in the hands of the vicious and the strong. Man will learn that poverty and want are due to the false conditions, the injustice which looks to human law and violence and force for its safeguard and protection. Man will learn that crime is but the hard profession that is left open to a large class of men by their avaricious fellows. When new opportunities for life are given, a fairer condition of existence will gradually be opened up and the need for violence and the cause of violence will disappear.

Instead of avenging a murder by taking a judge, sheriff, jurors, witnesses, jailer, hangman, and the various appendages of the court,—by taking these and staining their hands with blood and crime,—the world will make the original murder impossible, and thus save the crimes of all. Neither will the vicious control without the aid of law. Society ever has and must ever have a very large majority who naturally fall into order, social adjustment, and a rational, permissible means of life. The disorganized vicious would be far less powerful than the organized vicious, and would soon disappear.

Punishment to terrorize men from violating human order is like the threat of hell to terrorize souls into obedience to the law of God. Both mark primitive society, both are degrading and debasing, and can only appeal to the lower instincts of the lower class of men. Most religious teachers have ceased to win followers by threats of hell. Converts of this sort are not generally desired. The religion that does not approach and appeal to men along their higher conduct is not considered worthy to teach to man. And those souls who cannot be moved through the sentiments of justice and humanity, rather than threats of eternal fire, are very,

very rare, and even should such a soul exist the fear of hell would cause it still further to shrivel and decay.

Hatred, bitterness, violence and force can bring only bad results—they leave an evil stain on everyone they touch. No human soul can be rightly reached except through charity, humanity and love.

THE END.

Made in the USA
Las Vegas, NV
06 February 2022

43304190R00046